UNUSUAL CREATURES

A Mostly Accurate Account of Some of Earth's Strangest Animals

By MICHAEL HEARST

Artwork, Diagrams, and Other Visuals by
Arjen Noordeman, Christie Wright, and Jelmer Noordeman

chronicle books·san francisco

Library of Congress Cataloging-in-Publication Data
Hearst, Michael, 1972—
Unusual creatures : a mostly accurate account of some of Earth's strangest animals /
by Michael Hearst ; illustrations by Jelmer Noordeman.
p. cm.
ISBN 978-1-4521-0467-6 (alk. paper)
1. Animals—Miscellanea—Juvenile literature. I. Noordeman, Jelmer, ill. II. Title.

QL49.H495 2012
590—dc23

2011048646

Design by Arjen Noordeman and Christie Wright.
Typeset in Rockwell and Franklin Gothic.
The illustrations in this book were rendered in ink, with digitally applied color.

JELL-O is a registered trademark of Kraft Foods Holdings, Inc.
The Scotch brand and Scotch Tape are registered trademarks of 3M.

Manufactured in China.

1 3 5 7 9 10 8 6 4 2

Chronicle Books LLC
680 Second Street, San Francisco, California 94107

www.chroniclekids.com

CONTENTS

Michael Hearst
with one of his
unusual creature
instruments,
the claviola.

FROM THE AUTHOR

Who loves strange animals? Chances are *you* do if you bought this book. (Then again, perhaps your uncle gave it to you.) Whatever the case may be … my name is Michael Hearst, and I'd like to share with you some of my favorite unusual creatures. You ask, "What's an unusual creature?" Well, here's my definition…

un-u-su-al crea-ture (ən-'yü-zhə-wəl 'krē-chər) *noun.*
1. An animal that looks, sounds, smells, or acts in a way that makes you stop and say, "Whoa, dude! What's up with that?"

Truth be told, I love *all* animals. (If I had my way, I would have a pet giraffe that lived in my backyard; I would name it Ruth, and I would feed it acacia leaves from my second-floor bedroom window.) However, for these pages, we will focus on some of the lesser-known animals to roam the earth. I hope you have as much fun reading and looking through this book as I had putting it together. And I really hope at least a few of these unusual creatures make you stop and say, "Whoa, dude! What's up with that?"

—**Michael Hearst**

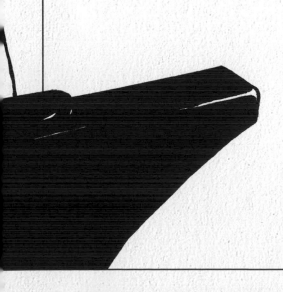

BIOLOGICAL CLASSIFICATIONS

IF YOU HAPPEN TO BE A BIOLOGIST (WHICH IS A SCIENTIST WHO STUDIES ANIMALS AND PLANTS AND THEIR RELATIONSHIP TO EVERYTHING AROUND THEM), YOU WILL WANT TO BREAK DOWN THE CLASSIFICATION OF EACH ANIMAL INTO THE FOLLOWING:

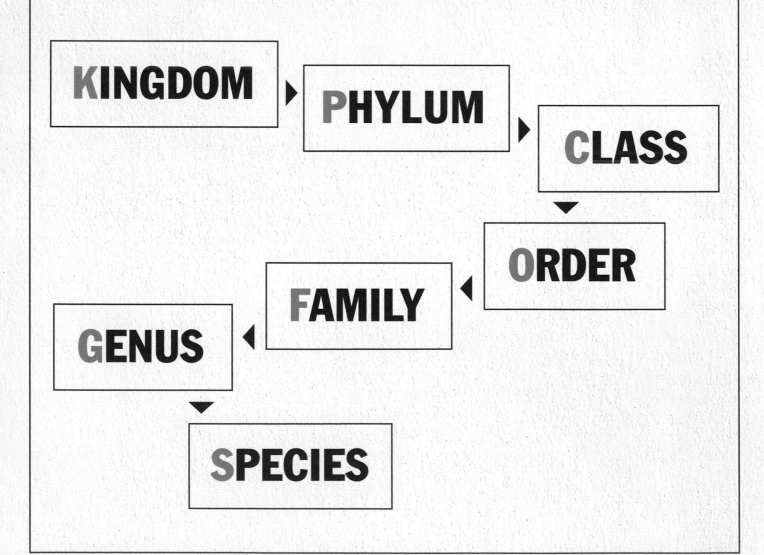

KINGDOM ▸ **PHYLUM** ▸ **CLASS** ▾ **ORDER** ◂ **FAMILY** ◂ **GENUS** ▾ **SPECIES**

You can memorize this
list by taking the first
letter of each category
and placing it in the
following mnemonic:
Kids Place Candles
On Foot Gravy Sausage.

TO FURTHER UNDERSTAND HOW THIS LIST WORKS,
LET'S LOOK AT THE DOMESTIC DOG AS AN EXAMPLE.

KINGDOM:	Animalia	An animal (i.e., not a plant).
PHYLUM:	Chordata	A vertebrate.
CLASS:	Mammalia	A mammal, which means it is air-breathing, has hair, and has three middle-ear bones.
ORDER:	Carnivora	A carnivore—it eats meat!
FAMILY:	Canidae	A wolf- or fox-like animal.
GENUS:	Canis	It is in the genus that houses coyotes, jackals, and wolves, among others.
SPECIES:	Canis lupus	The wolf species.
SUBSPECIES:	Canis lupus familiaris	And finally, here is the exact Latin term for the common domestic dog, descended from the wolf.

(YES, THERE CAN BE SUBSPECIES, AS WELL AS SUBGENERA, SUBPHYLA,
AND SUB- EVERYTHING ELSE. IT CAN GET COMPLICATED. MY APOLOGIES.)

Among the many CREATURES that roam the planet, there are two distinct categories: USUAL and UNUSUAL. Here are some examples of each:

USUAL	UNUSUAL
Squirrel	Three-Toed Sloth
Earthworm	Leafy Sea Dragon
Poodle	Star-Nosed Mole
Asian Elephant	Mimic Octopus
Tilapia	Chinese Giant Salamander
Amoeba	Dugong
Tiger	Olm
Field Mouse	Wombat
Pigeon	Giraffe-Necked Weevil
Dolphin	Slow Loris
Human	Magnapinna Squid
Cockroach	Tardigrade
Raccoon	Aye-aye
Hippopotamus	Tiburonia Granrojo
Littleneck Clam	Solenodon

Of course, all animals can also be categorized as vertebrates (with a backbone) or invertebrates (spineless).

VERTEBRATES

INVERTEBRATES

Did you know that *invertebrates* make up at least 95 percent of ALL animal species?

MAMMALS (*Mammalia*)
Such as dogs and monkeys.

PROTOZOA
Such as amoebas and flagellates.

BONY FISH (*Osteichthyes*)
Such as flounder and marlin.

INSECTS (*Insecta*)
Such as grasshoppers and ants.

AMPHIBIANS (*Amphibia*)
Such as frogs and salamanders.

ARACHNIDS (*Arachnida*)
Such as tarantulas and scorpions.

REPTILES (*Reptilia*)
Such as snakes and crocodiles.

BIVALVES (*Bivalvia*)
Such as clams, oysters, and mussels.

BIRDS (*Aves*)
Such as storks and pigeons.

CEPHALOPODS (*Cephalopoda*)
Such as octopuses, squid, and cuttlefish.

AND NOW YOU ARE ON YOUR WAY TO SPEAKING PERFECT LATIN!

AXOLOTL

KINGDOM	**Animalia**
PHYLUM	**Chordata**
CLASS	**Amphibia**
ORDER	**Caudata**
FAMILY	**Ambystomatidae**
GENUS	**Ambystoma**
SPECIES	**A. mexicanum**

SCIENTIFIC NAME: **AMBYSTOMA MEXICANUM**

''A'' is for axolotl. With external gills and wide smile, this salamander has been found in Central Mexico, specifically in two lakes: Lake Xochimilco and Lake Chalco. Sadly, Lake Chalco was drained over time to avoid flooding, and has been mostly paved over by streets, and Lake Xochimilco is much, much smaller than it ever used to be. Because of this, as well as pollution and the introduction of nonnative fish like tilapia and carp, which eat axolotls, this amphibian is now on the endangered-species list. Axolotls reach adulthood at 18 to 24 months, and can then live for another 10 to 15 years. Like other salamanders, the axolotl has the amazing ability to regenerate entire body parts. In some cases, axolotls have been known to regenerate a damaged limb and then grow an extra one!

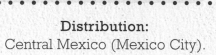

Distribution:
Central Mexico (Mexico City).

REGENERATION

Scientists are still investigating what enables the axolotl to regenerate body parts, including a leg, tail, eye, or even its heart! Although practical applications of this in human beings are still a long way off, researchers believe that what they learn from the axolotl might someday help humans to better heal from injuries—or, perhaps, help us to grow a tail.

amputation

bud

differentiation

complete

Fig. 1

AMPUTATE ▶ BUD ▶ DIFFERENTIATE ▶ REGENERATE!

Fig. 2 Axolotl

The name
axolotl comes from
the Aztec language.
The most common
translation is
"water dog."

AYE-AYE

KINGDOM	**Animalia**
PHYLUM	**Chordata**
CLASS	**Mammalia**
ORDER	**Primates**
FAMILY	**Daubentoniidae**
GENUS	**Daubentonia**
SPECIES	**D.madagascariensis**

SCIENTIFIC NAME: DAUBENTONIA MADAGASCARIENSIS

This nocturnal primate is native to Madagascar. Its special features include rodent-like teeth and a long, thin middle finger. It uses the finger to tap on trees in search of hollow sounds. When it finds one, it gnaws a hole in the wood and then inserts its elongated finger to pull out the insect larvae.

A Brief and Happy Story

Evidence has recently shown that aye-ayes may not be as threatened as previously believed, thanks to conservationists like the Duke Lemur Center (where you can visit aye-ayes, and also purchase a stuffed-animal aye-aye to snuggle with in bed!).

Fig. 3 Aye-aye tapping on a tree to find food.

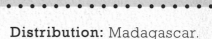

Distribution: Madagascar.

A Brief and Sad Story

Unfortunately, some native people of Madagascar believe that the aye-aye is an evil omen—a superstitious symbol of death—and will go out of their way to kill this poor creature.

Outside of Madagascar, the aye-aye is a rare sight. However, if you travel to the Denver Zoo, the San Francisco Zoo, or the Duke Lemur Center in Durham, North Carolina (as I did), you are likely to find this amazing creature.

Did you know?

Aye-ayes are the only primates known to use echolocation to find prey. They locate food by tapping on trees and carefully listening to the sound of the echo.

Fig. 4 Aye-aye

Inches 1 2 3 4 5 6 7 8 9 10 11 12 13 14 15 16 17 18 19 20 21 22

BAR-HEADED GOOSE

SCIENTIFIC NAME: ANSER INDICUS

The bar-headed goose is found, in groups of thousands, in central Asia, where it migrates long distances every year from one climate to another, just like many other birds. The difference, however, with this unusual creature, is that it makes its journey over the Himalayas, which rise to 29,029 feet! At this altitude, winds soar up to 200 miles per hour, and the air is so thin that helicopters cannot fly (though you probably would not want to fly a helicopter in 200-mile-per-hour winds, anyway). The temperature is also cold enough to freeze skin instantly. So how (and why) does the bar-headed goose do this? It does it to avoid the summer monsoons of India. (It also makes the return trip in the fall to avoid the wintry storms of Tibet.) The fastest, most direct route just happens to be over the Himalayan Mountains. Fortunately for the bar-headed goose, it has a number of special features to help with this challenging journey. It has a larger wing size relative to its weight than most birds. This goose also has more capillaries and more efficient red blood cells than other birds, which means that it can get oxygen to its muscles' cells much more quickly. And perhaps my favorite tidbit of information: the bar-headed goose can breathe incredibly fast without getting dizzy or passing out, which certainly comes in handy when there's not a whole lot of oxygen. And if all that's not impressive enough, a recent study was conducted to see exactly how long it takes the bar-headed goose to make this incredible migration. It appears that the goose flew its Himalayan portion of the trip in a single effort that took just about 8 hours, with no rest.

KINGDOM	Animalia
PHYLUM	Chordata
CLASS	Aves
ORDER	Anseriformes
FAMILY	Anatidae
GENUS	Anser
SPECIES	A. indicus

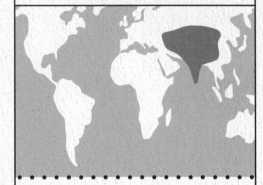

Distribution:
Central Asia and southern Asia, as far south as India.

The bird setting the record for highest flight was a Rüppell's griffon. This enormous vulture (which can have a wingspan of up to 10 feet) was soaring 37,000 feet above the Ivory Coast of Africa when it had the misfortune of getting sucked into the jet engine of an airplane. The plane was damaged, but landed safely. The vulture was not so lucky.

Did you know?

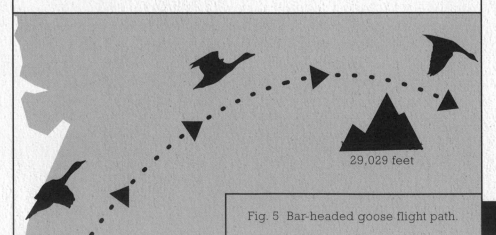

29,029 feet

Fig. 5 Bar-headed goose flight path.

Fig. 6 Bar-Headed Goose

Feet   1   2

BARKING SPIDER
(EASTERN TARANTULA)

SCIENTIFIC NAME: **SELENOCOSMIA CRASSIPES**

KINGDOM	**Animalia**
PHYLUM	**Arthropoda**
CLASS	**Arachnida**
ORDER	**Araneae**
FAMILY	**Theraphosidae**
GENUS	**Selenocosmia**
SPECIES	**S. crassipes**

Okay, so it doesn't actually bark. But it does make a distinct sound when provoked. Not to mention the barking spider's bite can cause up to 6 hours of vomiting. Not exactly the way I want to spend an afternoon. These tarantulas commonly prey on insects, lizards, frogs, mice, and even small birds.

OVERLY SENSATIONALIZED NEWS REPORT

In 2009, British newspapers such as the *Times* and the *Telegraph* reported, "Giant spiders invade Australian Outback town." Apparently, the town of Bowen, nearly 700 miles northwest of Brisbane, was being overrun with "scores of eastern tarantulas." The article continued, "The 'bird-eating spiders'. . . have begun crawling out from gardens and venturing into public spaces." Local pest controller Audy Geiszler warned people "to make sure they [wore] shoes and gloves when they are gardening." The spiders "are not deadly but can make humans extremely ill and kill large domestic animals with one bite." It was later revealed that only 10 spiders had been sighted.

Distribution:
East coast of Australia.

I've been told:

The term *barking spider* is also a reference to audible flatulence. "Wasn't me. Must have been those barking spiders!" However, I've never actually heard anyone use this term, and I live in a very urban environment where flatulence happens quite frequently.

Fig. 7 Barking Spider
(Eastern Tarantula)

Inches   1   2   3   4   5   6

BEE HUMMINGBIRD

KINGDOM	**Animalia**
PHYLUM	**Chordata**
CLASS	**Aves**
ORDER	**Trochiliformes**
FAMILY	**Trochilidae**
GENUS	**Mellisuga**
SPECIES	**M. helenae**

SCIENTIFIC NAME: **MELLISUGA HELENAE**

Measuring just 2 inches in length and weighing under 2 grams, the bee hummingbird is the smallest bird in the world! (At least, the male is. Females are slightly larger.) Found in Cuba, these mini birds can easily be mistaken for insects. Their wings flap so rapidly (an average of 80 beats per second) that the human eye can only see a blur. And just to add to its high-energy antics, the bee hummingbird can fly up to 20 hours nonstop. Perhaps this hard work is why they drink 8 times their total body mass each day. (Sort of like if you or I drank four bathtubs full of water every day.) The bee hummingbird feeds mainly on nectar. Their tongues are shaped like drinking straws, allowing them to easily pull nectar from flowers. While doing this, the bird also picks up pollen on its bill and head, which it then transfers from flower to flower. Because of this, the bee hummingbird plays a very important role in plant reproduction. In just one day it may visit 1,500 flowers. Thank you, bee hummingbird!

Distribution:
Cuba and the
Isla de la Juventud.

Fig. 8 Bee Hummingbird

Inches   1

WHICH ONE IS *NOT* TRUE?

1. Bee hummingbirds have an incredibly fast heart rate of up to 1,200 beats per minute—second place only to the Etruscan shrew, which has a rate of up to 1,511 beats per minute.

2. In Cuba, people call the bird *zunzuncito*, which loosely means "little buzz buzz" in Spanish.

3. The bee hummingbird carries a venomous sting, which, when mixed with alcohol, can impair one's ability to drive.

4. The bee hummingbird's eggs are about the size of your smallest fingernail.

Answers: Indeed, number 3 is not true. The bee hummingbird does not sting. Of course, alcohol on its own can easily impair your judgment and ability to drive. So don't drink and drive.

BILBY

KINGDOM	Animalia
PHYLUM	Chordata
CLASS	Mammalia
ORDER	Peramelemorphia
FAMILY	Thylacomyidae
GENUS	Macrotis
SPECIES	M. lagotis

SCIENTIFIC NAME: MACROTIS LAGOTIS

Found only in Australia, the bilby is a small, nocturnal marsupial. The young stay in their mother's backward-tilting pouch for 70 to 80 days. The name *bilby* comes from the Aboriginal language of northern New South Wales, and means "long-nosed rat." Bilbies do not need to drink water; they get all the water they need from their food, which includes fruit, seeds, insects, and small animals.

Distribution:
Northwestern and central Australia.

THE BILBY: A SHORT POEM

*Not a long-nosed rat,
the bilby is in fact a mini marsupial.
The female has a pouch, which faces backward—
rather unusual.
This keeps the pouch from filling with dirt
as she digs into the ground.
The desert of Queensland and northern Australia
is where this creature can be found.
The bilby's eyes are poor at seeing far or seeing near.
Fortunately for the bilby,
its strength lies in its ability to hear.*

Fig. 9 The bilby's pouch and the kangaroo's pouch.

In Australia, the bilby has become a popular alternative to the Easter Bunny. Look out! Here comes the Easter Bilby!

Did you know?

The female bilby's pouch faces the opposite direction from that of the kangaroo's. This prevents her pouch from filling with dirt while she is burrowing.

Fig. 10 Bilby

BLOBFISH

KINGDOM	**Animalia**
PHYLUM	**Chordata**
CLASS	**Actinopterygii**
ORDER	**Scorpaeniformes**
FAMILY	**Psychrolutidae**
GENUS	**Psychrolutes**
SPECIES	**P. marcidus**

SCIENTIFIC NAME: **PSYCHROLUTES MARCIDUS**

The blobfish is a blobular fish that lives off the coasts of Tasmania and mainland Australia at depths of up to 2,500 feet. At this depth the water pressure is quite extreme. Fortunately for the blobfish, it is made of a jellylike substance that is less dense than water, which allows it to float rather comfortably just above the ocean floor. The drawback is that the blobfish hardly has a muscle in its body, and without muscles the blobfish is worthless at hunting for food. Instead, it simply sits around and waits for the food to float into its mouth. Blobfish!

Distribution: Off the coasts of mainland Australia and Tasmania.

Fig. 11 Blobfish

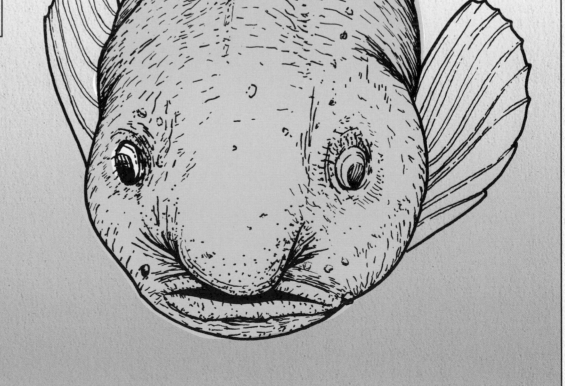

Inches 1 2 3 4 5 6 7 8 9

Fig. 12

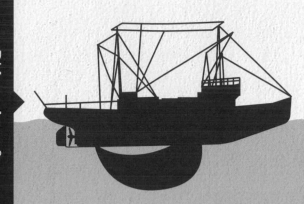

The blobfish

is currently facing extinction due to fishing trawlers, which drag nets along the seafloor and catch way more stuff than they actually need to catch. Totally lame, fishing trawlers!

THE BLOBFISH: A SHORT POEM

Blobfish, blobfish JELL-O of the sea—
Floats upon the bottom, lazy as can be.
Hardly has a muscle, but doesn't seem to mind.
It eats what floats into its mouth—crustaceans and some brine.
And yes, it has a saddened look; perhaps it's feeling down—
For, thanks to fishing trawlers
Soon this fish won't be around.

Fig. 13 Blobfish, front view on land.

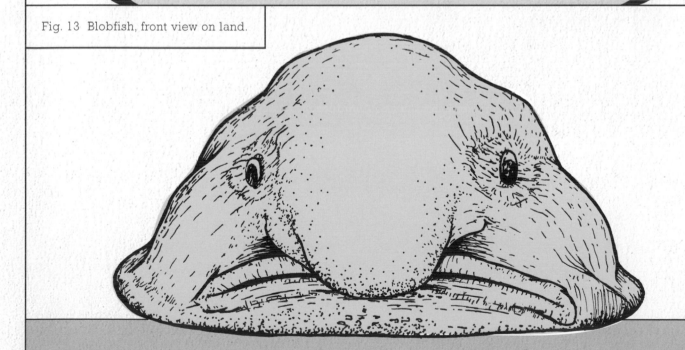

Blobfish: not as cute as the aye-aye.

BLUE-FOOTED BOOBY

SCIENTIFIC NAME: **SULA NEBOUXII**

The blue-footed booby is a long-winged sea bird with a set of magnificently colored feet. These unusual birds often dive for their food from altitudes of up to 300 feet, at speeds of 60 miles per hour, and can swim to depths of 80 feet below the water's surface. When a male blue-footed booby attempts to impress a female, he flaunts his colorful feet and performs a dance by spreading his wings and stamping on the ground. I call this dance the blue-footed boogaloo.

KINGDOM	**Animalia**
PHYLUM	**Chordata**
CLASS	**Aves**
ORDER	**Pelecaniformes**
FAMILY	**Sulidae**
GENUS	**Sula**
SPECIES	**S. nebouxii**

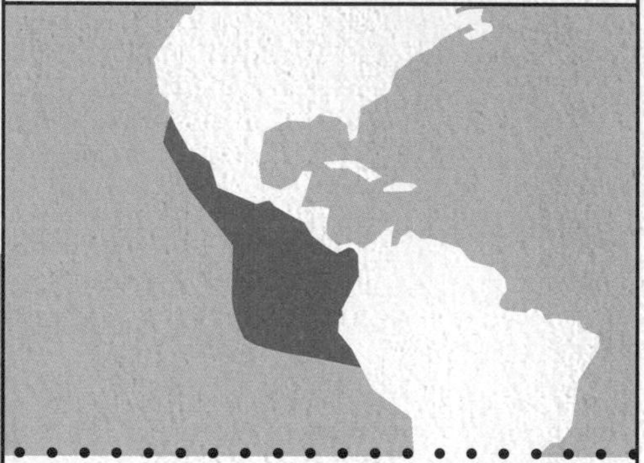

300 feet

80 feet

Fig. 14 The blue-footed booby can dive down more than 80 feet!

Did you know?

Distribution: West coast of Southern California, Mexico, Central America, and northern South America.

TRUE OR TRUE?

1   The female blue-footed booby also has blue feet, but not nearly as striking as the male's.

2   During courtship, females are likely to select the males with the brightest feet.

3   The name *booby* is thought to originate from the Spanish word *bobo*, which means "clown."

4   The booby's nostrils are permanently closed so that it can easily dive and swim underwater.

5   Special air sacs in the booby's skull protect its brain from the constant high impact of diving.

Answers: 1.T 2.T 3.T 4.T 5.T

Special
air sac
for padding

Permanently
closed
nostrils

There is a distinct possibility
that the term *booby trap* derives
from a rope trap that sailors
would use to try and catch this
sea bird.

Fig. 15 Blue-Footed Booby

CANTOR'S GIANT SOFT-SHELLED TURTLE

SCIENTIFIC NAME: **PELOCHELYS CANTORII**

Also called the frog-head turtle or the Asian giant soft-shelled turtle, this freshwater turtle can be easily recognized by its broad head with eyes close to the tip of its snout, its soft shell, and, oh, yeah, its 6-foot span from head to tail. Instead of a typical exterior shell, this creature has rubbery skin. In order to keep itself safe from predators, it spends quite a bit of time buried in the sand. In fact, it spends 95 percent of its life hidden and motionless, with only its eyes and nose peeking out. Unfortunately, that hasn't been enough protection to keep it from becoming highly endangered.

KINGDOM	**Animalia**
PHYLUM	**Chordata**
CLASS	**Sauropsida**
ORDER	**Testudines**
FAMILY	**Trionychidae**
GENUS	**Pelochelys**
SPECIES	**P. cantorii**

Distribution:
Southeast Asia.

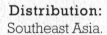

FIVE NOTES OF INTEREST

1 The Cantor's giant soft-shelled turtle has large, powerful claws. It can also extend its neck faster than you can say the word "cobra," giving it one of the fastest strikes of any animal.

2 Endangerment of this turtle is largely due to pollution, habitat loss, and illegal hunting and fishing of the species. Apparently giant soft-shelled turtle is a delicacy in Vietnam. Boo!

3 At the time of writing this section, Cambodian monks (in partnership with the United States–based Conservation International) were opening a new conservation center to help save giant soft-shelled turtles from extinction. Yay for Cambodian monks!

4 The Cantor's giant soft-shelled turtle is named after a 19th-century Danish botanist and officer in the Bengal Medical Service, Dr. Theodore Edward Cantor. He is lucky enough to also have his name attached to the Cantor's dusky leaf monkey and the Cantor's roundleaf bat.

5 I've just decided to rename Maddie (my tortoiseshell cat). She is now Hearst's soft-furred tortoiseshell cat.

Fig. 16 The giant soft-shelled turtle possesses long claws.

Fig. 17 Cantor's Giant Soft-Shelled Turtle

This **turtle** may have a rubbery shell, but its jaws are powerful enough to crush bone.

7

6

5

4

3

2

1

Feet

KINGDOM	Animalia
PHYLUM	Chordata
CLASS	Amphibia
ORDER	Caudata
FAMILY	Cryptobranchidae
GENUS	Andrias
SPECIES	A. davidianus

CHINESE

SCIENTIFIC NAME: **ANDRIAS DAVIDIANUS**

The Chinese giant salamander is the largest salamander in the world, reaching a length as long as 6 feet. Next in line would be its slightly smaller cousin, the Japanese giant salamander. With its bulbous head, small eyes, and wrinkly skin, this massive amphibian feeds on insects, frogs, and fish.

Distribution:
China.

Did you know?

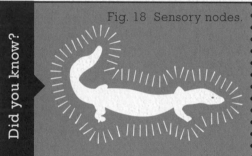

Fig. 18 Sensory nodes.

The Chinese giant salamander has very poor eyesight. Instead it relies on sensory nodes that extend from the creature's head to its tail, and which can detect the slightest vibrations.

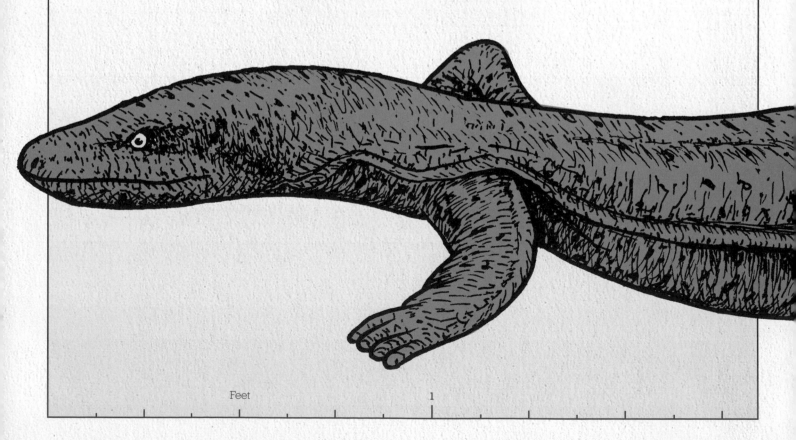

Feet   1

GIANT SALAMANDER

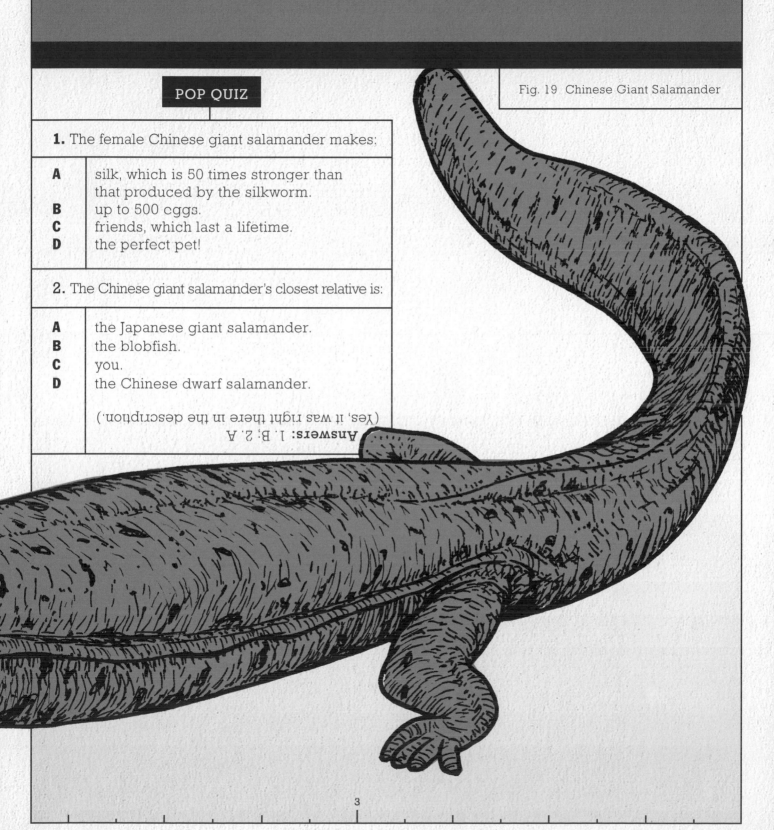

POP QUIZ

1. The female Chinese giant salamander makes:

A silk, which is 50 times stronger than that produced by the silkworm.
B up to 500 cggs.
C friends, which last a lifetime.
D the perfect pet!

2. The Chinese giant salamander's closest relative is:

A the Japanese giant salamander.
B the blobfish.
C you.
D the Chinese dwarf salamander.

Answers: 1. B. 2. A
(Yes, it was right there in the description.)

DUGONG

SCIENTIFIC NAME: **DUGONG DUGON**

Long ago, the ancestors of the dugong lived on land. Now this large marine mammal can be found grazing on underwater plants and grasses, many of which also lived on dry land at one time. Like giant vacuum cleaners, dugongs hover over underwater pastures off the coast of northern Australia, Southeast Asia, and the east coast of Africa. These giant vegetarians, also referred to as "sea cows," are surprisingly more closely related to elephants than to other marine mammals like whales and dolphins. Their closest living aquatic relatives are the manatees.

KINGDOM	**Animalia**
PHYLUM	**Chordata**
CLASS	**Mammalia**
ORDER	**Sirenia**
FAMILY	**Dugongidae**
GENUS	**Dugong**
SPECIES	**D. dugon**

Distribution: Warm coastal waters from the Pacific Ocean to the coast of Africa.

As mammals, dugongs must breathe air. Because they spend much of their time in shallow waters, dugongs sometimes breathe by standing on their tails with their heads above water, just like we do in the shallow end of a pool . . . except for the tail part.

Feet   1   2   3   4

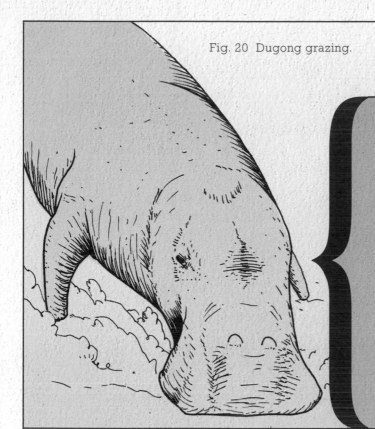

Fig. 20 Dugong grazing.

A SHORT POEM ABOUT THE DUGONG

In the waters of Australia,
in the shallows of Moreton Bay,
you can find the last living members
of the family Dugongidae.
A bulbous beast, the dugong
is a mammal of the sea.
Its fusiform body is similar
in shape to that of a manatee.
The snout is sharply downturned
so it can graze upon the floor;
it vacuums up the sea grasses . . .
and perhaps a little more.

Fig. 21 Dugong

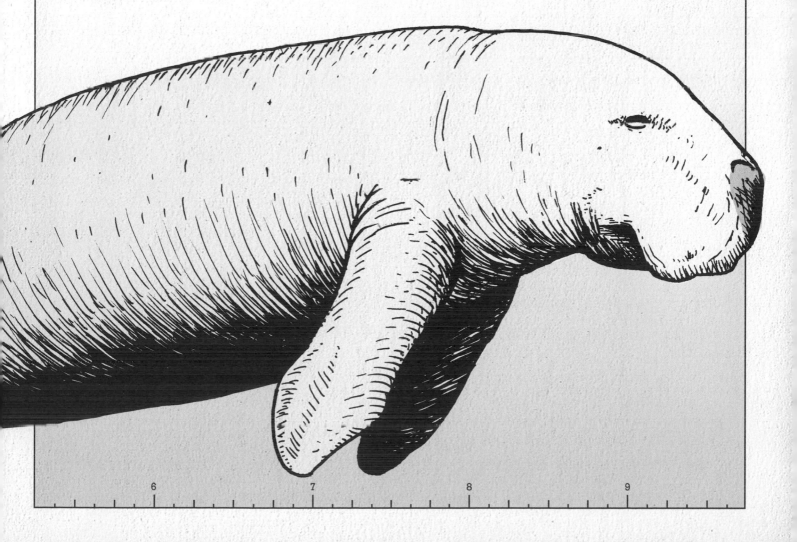

ECHIDNA

SCIENTIFIC NAME: **TACHYGLOSSUS ACULEATUS (AND OTHERS)**

Echidnas (along with platypuses) are among the elite few mammals that lay eggs. Like a porcupine or hedgehog, the echidna is covered with coarse hairs and sharp spines. Another prominent feature on this unusual creature is its long snout, which functions as both mouth and nose. This unusual creature, with its muscular legs and long claws, is a fantastic digger and can easily tear open a log to get at termites. It then uses its long, sticky tongue to remove the insects. Slurp!

KINGDOM	**Animalia**
PHYLUM	**Chordata**
CLASS	**Mammalia**
ORDER	**Monotremata**
FAMILY	**Tachyglossidae**
GENUS	**Various**
SPECIES	**Various**

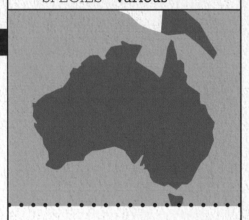

Distribution:
New Guinea and Australia.

TRUE OR TRUE?

1   The echidna is named after a monster in ancient Greek mythology.

2   Because the mother has no nipples, baby echidnas suck milk from pores on the mother's "milk patch." This is also true of the platypus.

3   The baby echidna is born no bigger than a jelly bean.

4   Echidnas are rather shy, and when threatened, will roll up into a tight ball.

Answers: 1.T 2.T 3.T 4.T

Fig. 22 The name *echidna* originates from the Greek goddess Echidna who was believed to have the face of a woman and the body of a serpent.

Did you know?

Fig. 23 A young echidna is called a puggle.

Fig. 24 Echidna

ELEPHANT SHREW

SCIENTIFIC NAME: **RHYNCHOCYON PETERSI (AND OTHERS)**

It's true, it's true, there's an elephant shrew. Surprisingly, however, the elephant shrew is not related to the shrew at all. Its genetic makeup is actually closer to that of manatees, aardvarks, and, surprisingly, elephants. These small insect-eaters can be found in a variety of habitats: from deserts and grasslands to coastal bush forests.

KINGDOM	**Animalia**
PHYLUM	**Chordata**
CLASS	**Mammalia**
ORDER	**Macroscelidea**
FAMILY	**Macroscelididea**
GENUS	**Various**
SPECIES	**Various**

Fig. 25 Elephant Shrew.

Even though **elephant shrews** do not typically like each other, they often live in pairs to better defend their territory . . . however, they still sleep in separate nests.

Inches 1 2 3 4 5 6 7 8 9 10 11 12 13

THE ELEPHANT SHREW: 4 FUN FACTS

1   There are 17 known living species of elephant shrew, including the short-eared elephant shrew, the dusky-footed elephant shrew, and, my favorite, the golden-rumped elephant shrew.

2   Biologists often refer to this animal by its African name, *sengi*, to keep it from being confused with the actual shrew, which comes from an entirely different family.

3   The elephant shrew is extremely quick, and can leap up to 3 feet.

4   Elephant shrews are very careful not to get caught by predators, and will often clear an emergency escape route, just in case a threat comes their way.

Fig. 26 The elephant shrew uses its nose to find food.

Did you know?

Distribution:
Southern Africa and parts of northern Africa.

Fig. 27 The elephant shrew is about $^1/_{13}$ the size of an African elephant.

FLYING SNAKE

SCIENTIFIC NAME: **CHRYSOPELEA PARADISI (AND OTHERS)**

There are five known species of flying snake, all of which are found in Asia between India and Indonesia. Unfortunately, none of them can *actually* fly. They can, however, launch themselves from trees and glide through the air for distances of over 300 feet (longer than a football field). To do this, the flying snake will slither to the end of a branch and dangle itself in a J shape. Then, pushing off from the branch, the snake quickly changes to an S shape. While airborne, the snake sucks in its stomach, flattening and widening itself to twice its normal width. This gives its body a concave shape, which can trap air, allowing it to glide to its destination. There have been no reports of flying snakes landing on people's heads. Yet.

KINGDOM	**Animalia**
PHYLUM	**Chordata**
CLASS	**Sauropsida**
ORDER	**Squamata**
FAMILY	**Colubridae**
GENUS	**Chrysopelea**
SPECIES	**Various**

Distribution: Southeast Asia (the mainland, Greater and Lesser Sundas, Maluku, and the Philippines), southernmost China, India, Sri Lanka, and Indonesia.

OPERATION FLYING SNAKE

In 2010, the *Washington Post* reported that the U.S. Department of Defense (DOD) had set out to try to uncover the secrets of the flying snake. In particular, a researcher from Virginia Tech had been funded by the DOD to travel to Asia and analyze the way these snakes can sail through the air from tree to tree. The *Washington Post* tried to find out more from the DOD, but the government chose not to respond.

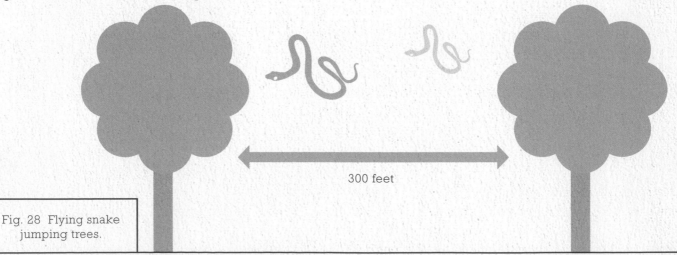

300 feet

Fig. 28 Flying snake jumping trees.

Fig. 29 Flying Snake

The
flying snake
creates air resistance
while in flight by
flattening itself
and becoming
wider.

Inches

KINGDOM	**Animalia**
PHYLUM	**Chordata**
CLASS	**Mammalia**
ORDER	**Pilosa**
FAMILY	**Myrmecophagidae**
GENUS	**Myrmecophaga**
SPECIES	**M. tridactyla**

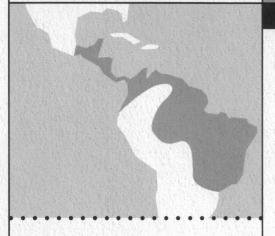

Distribution:
Northeastern South America and Central America.

Did you know?

The giant anteater can flick its 2-foot-long tongue up to 150 times per minute, consuming up to 30,000 ants in a single day.

Fig. 30 Giant Anteater

GIANT

SCIENTIFIC NAME: **MYRMECOPHAGA TRIDACTYLA**

The giant anteater is the largest species of anteater, reaching sizes of up to 7 feet in length, and weighing between 60 and 140 pounds. Although this animal has no teeth, it uses its sharp claws to open anthills. Then, with its long snout and tongue, it quickly laps up as many ants as possible before taking a break from the painful ant stings. It should be mentioned here that anteaters never destroy anthills. That way they can come back later for *more* ants.

Feet   1   2   3

ANTEATER

SURE, BUT DID YOU KNOW THAT . . .

... **giant anteaters** walk on their knuckles to protect their long front claws?

... **giant anteaters** are solitary creatures, with the exception of the newborn, which rides on its mother's back?

... **baby anteaters** line up the stripes on their fur exactly with their mother's stripes? Scientists are not sure why they do this. Perhaps to make the baby hard for predators to spot?

... **the giant anteater** sleeps as much as 15 hours per day? It also uses its long, bushy tail as a blanket.

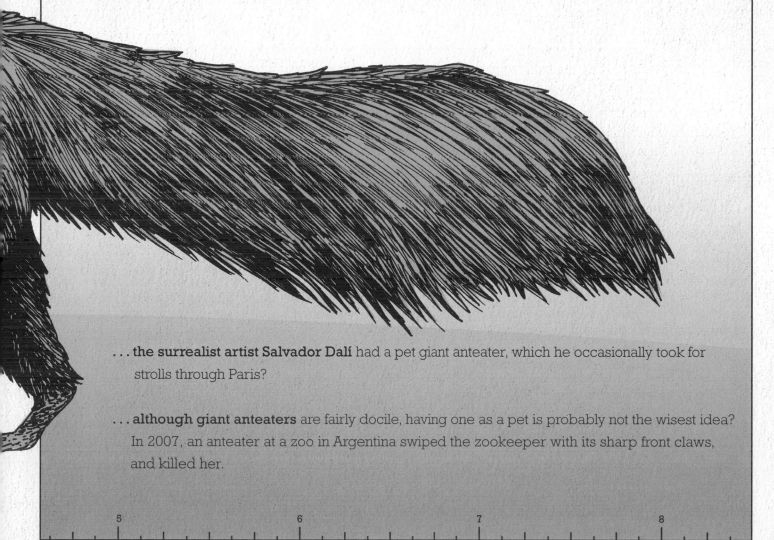

... **the surrealist artist Salvador Dalí** had a pet giant anteater, which he occasionally took for strolls through Paris?

... **although giant anteaters** are fairly docile, having one as a pet is probably not the wisest idea? In 2007, an anteater at a zoo in Argentina swiped the zookeeper with its sharp front claws, and killed her.

GIANT GIPPSLAND EARTHWORM

SCIENTIFIC NAME: MEGASCOLIDES AUSTRALIS

No, it's not a snake. It's a giant earthworm! And of course, it's from Australia, where so many other unusual creatures live. The giant Gippsland earthworm, with its purple head and bluish body, averages 3 feet long and 1 inch in diameter. These massive earthworms live in deep burrows along streams and hills in Gippsland, Australia. Like most earthworms, they require plenty of water to stay alive. The moisture is needed to transport oxygen from the outside air into their bodies (similar to breathing, but not quite breathing). Because of this need to stay moist, these worms hardly ever leave their homes. Compared to other invertebrates, they have long life spans and can take 5 years to mature, at which point they have been known to reach lengths of 10 feet. In the warmer months, breeding takes place, and the worms lay large egg cocoons in their burrows. Twelve months later, when the worms hatch, they are already more than 6 inches long.

KINGDOM	**Animalia**
PHYLUM	**Annelida**
CLASS	**Oligochaeta**
ORDER	**Opisthopora**
FAMILY	**Megascolecidae**
GENUS	**Megascolides**
SPECIES	**M. australis**

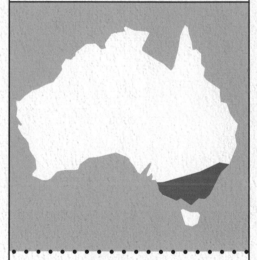

Distribution:
Gippsland, Australia.

WILDLIFE WONDERLAND'S GIANT EARTHWORM MUSEUM

Not surprisingly, there is a Giant Earthworm Museum in Gippsland, Australia. Inside the museum you can see plenty of giant earthworms, and even crawl through a magnified replica of a worm burrow, as well as an even more magnified replica of an earthworm's stomach. Apparently, next to Wildlife Wonderland's Giant Earthworm Museum is Wildlife Wonderland's Wombat World. Try saying that 5 times fast.

The largest earthworm ever reported was not one of these.

It was a giant South African earthworm, measuring 22 feet long.

Did you know?

Fig. 31 Giant Gippsland Earthworm

standard
earthworm

giant
Gippsland
earthworm

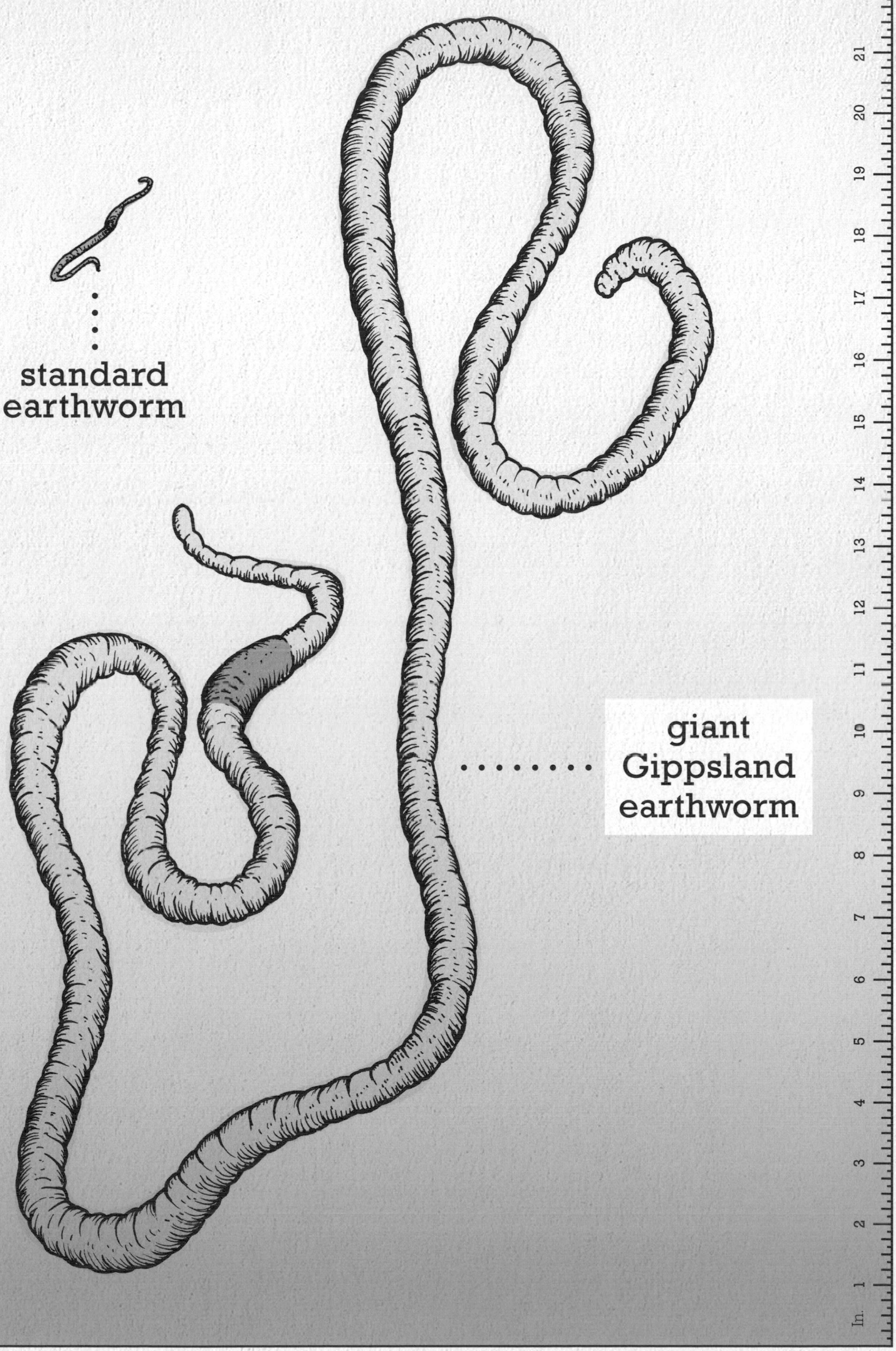

GIRAFFE-NECKED WEEVIL

SCIENTIFIC NAME: **TRACHELOPHORUS GIRAFFA**

I love giraffes, and would have included them in this book, but as I pointed out in the introduction, the giraffe would need to go in a book of "usual" creatures. Thankfully, however, there is the giraffe-necked weevil, found only on the island of Madagascar. The neck of the male giraffe-necked weevil is about 2 or 3 times the length of the female's neck, and the entire body length of this weevil is typically under an inch. The male uses its extended neck to fight with other males, at which point they look somewhat like two excavator construction vehicles at war. The winner gets the big prize . . . the female giraffe-necked weevil! In turn, the female will use her neck and powerful legs to fold a leaf in half, and then curl up one end. Inside the curl, she will lay a single egg, and will then continue rolling up the leaf into a tight cigar shape. This helps protect the egg while it incubates. Quite a bit of work!

KINGDOM	**Animalia**
PHYLUM	**Arthropoda**
CLASS	**Insecta**
ORDER	**Coleoptera**
FAMILY	**Attelabidae**
GENUS	**Trachelophorus**
SPECIES	**T. giraffa**

Distribution: Madagascar.

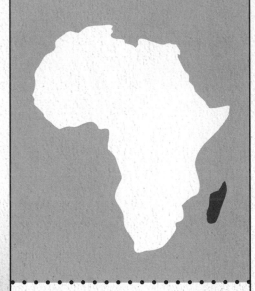

Fig. 32 Weevil laying an egg.

Fig. 33 · Giraffe-Necked Weevil

A **weevil** is a beetle. Beetles make up about 40 percent of all insects on the planet.

The Beatles, a British rock band from the '60s, make up about 40 percent of all music played on oldies radio.

Inches   ½

GLASS FROG

KINGDOM	**Animalia**
PHYLUM	**Chordata**
CLASS	**Amphibia**
ORDER	**Anura**
FAMILY	**Centrolenidae**
GENUS	**Various**
SPECIES	**Various**

SCIENTIFIC NAME: **COCHRANELLA SPINOSA (AND OTHERS)**

This tiny nocturnal frog has see-through skin on its belly and chest, which allows you to observe its inner organs. Glass frogs are typically quite small, ranging from 1 to 3 inches. They live in the trees and plants of rain forests in Central and South America, often in cloud forests. (A cloud forest is a rain forest at the top of a mountain in the clouds.) Because of this, the glass frog is very difficult to find. Of course, the glass frog probably doesn't want to be found.

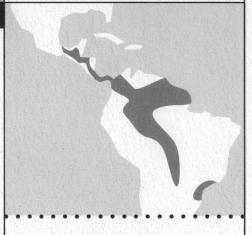

Distribution:
Rain forests of Central and South America.

Did you know?

1 In most cases, you can see the glass frog's liver, digestive tract, lungs, and sometimes the heart beating through its skin.

2 There are believed to be at least 138 species of glass frogs.

3 Glass frogs often lay their eggs on leaves that overhang water pools. When the eggs hatch, the tadpoles drop into the water.

4 Glass frogs are occasionally found hiding in kitchen cabinets next to dishes and bowls. (Okay, I made that up. It's not true.)

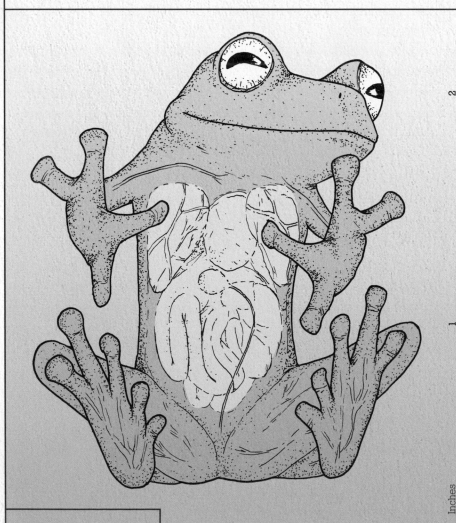

Inches

Fig. 34 Glass Frog

GREAT HORNBILL

KINGDOM	**Animalia**
PHYLUM	**Chordata**
CLASS	**Aves**
ORDER	**Coraciiformes**
FAMILY	**Bucerotidae**
GENUS	**Buceros**
SPECIES	**B. bicornis**

SCIENTIFIC NAME: BUCEROS BICORNIS

The great hornbill is a fruit-loving bird found in parts of Southeast Asia. It prominently features a golden-yellow helmet (called a casque) on the top of its head. This casque acts as a resonating chamber to amplify the bird's super-loud calls. (It also proves that the bird is a mature adult—the casque takes 5 years to develop to its full size.) Perhaps the most unusual feature of the great hornbill, however, is the manner in which it raises its young. After a courtship ritual, which includes wing and tail displays and beating of bills on the ground, the pair will spend several days choosing just the right hollowed-out section of a tree for the female to build her nest. The hornbill pair will then seal the entrance to the tree with mud and poop until the female is completely imprisoned within. Here she will remain for up to 4 months while raising her chicks. All the while, the male will bring her whole or regurgitated food, feeding her through a small slit in the entrance. The female also keeps the nest clean by dropping her waste through the small opening for the male to take away. Soon after the chicks are hatched, the mother leaves the nest, and the chicks reseal the entrance behind her. At this point, Mom and Dad both bring food to the chicks until they are ready to take off.

Distribution: India, the Malay Peninsula, and Sumatra, Indonesia.

Fig. 35 Great Hornbill

Did you know?

Zoos and conservation programs have sent artificial fiberglass beaks and the tail feathers from captive hornbills to tribes in Borneo and India to try and prevent them from killing wild hornbills for dress and ceremonial purposes.

Feet 1 2 3 4

GUINEAFOWL PUFFERFISH

KINGDOM	Animalia
PHYLUM	Chordata
CLASS	Actinopterygii
ORDER	Tetraodontiformes
FAMILY	Tetraodontidae
GENUS	Arothron
SPECIES	A. meleagris

SCIENTIFIC NAME: AROTHRON MELEAGRIS

Did you know there are at least 189 species of pufferfish in the world? I have chosen the guineafowl pufferfish for this book because it's the most ridiculous-looking of them all. Also known as balloonfish, blowfish, bubblefish, globefish, swellfish, toadfish, honey toads, and sugar toads, these fish all have the unique ability to quickly change their size from that of a normal-looking fish to that of a rather bulbous and extremely pointy ball. Needless to say, this is a defense mechanism to avoid being eaten by predators. In case that's not enough of a deterrent, the pufferfish also happens to be one of the most poisonous vertebrates on the planet (only second to the golden poison frog). In particular, the fish's liver, ovaries, and skin are highly toxic. Predators who try to chomp on a puffer will be lucky if all they get is a perforated tongue.

FOUR COMMON MISCONCEPTIONS ABOUT THE PUFFERFISH, DEBUNKED

1 Pufferfish did not first learn how to puff themselves into a ball after repeatedly watching the Violet Beauregarde scene in the movie *Willy Wonka & the Chocolate Factory* (the original 1971 film, that is).

2 The esteemed rapper Puff Daddy (a.k.a. P. Diddy) is not one of the foremost authorities on pufferfish.

3 Pufferfish are not hired to entertain other young fish at birthday parties, performing magic tricks and making balloon animals, such as pufferfish.

4 Pufferfish do not like to occasionally puff on a corncob pipe after a delicious meal.

Note: Pufferfish don't smoke. Neither should you!

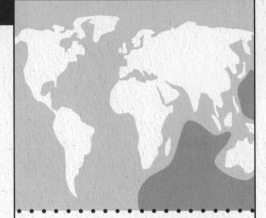

Distribution:
Indo- and Eastern Pacific.

Fugu is the Japanese word for pufferfish, which is considered a delicacy. If not prepared properly, it may be the last piece of sashimi you ever eat.

Did you know?

Fig. 36 Before and after puffing.

Fig. 37 Guineafowl Pufferfish

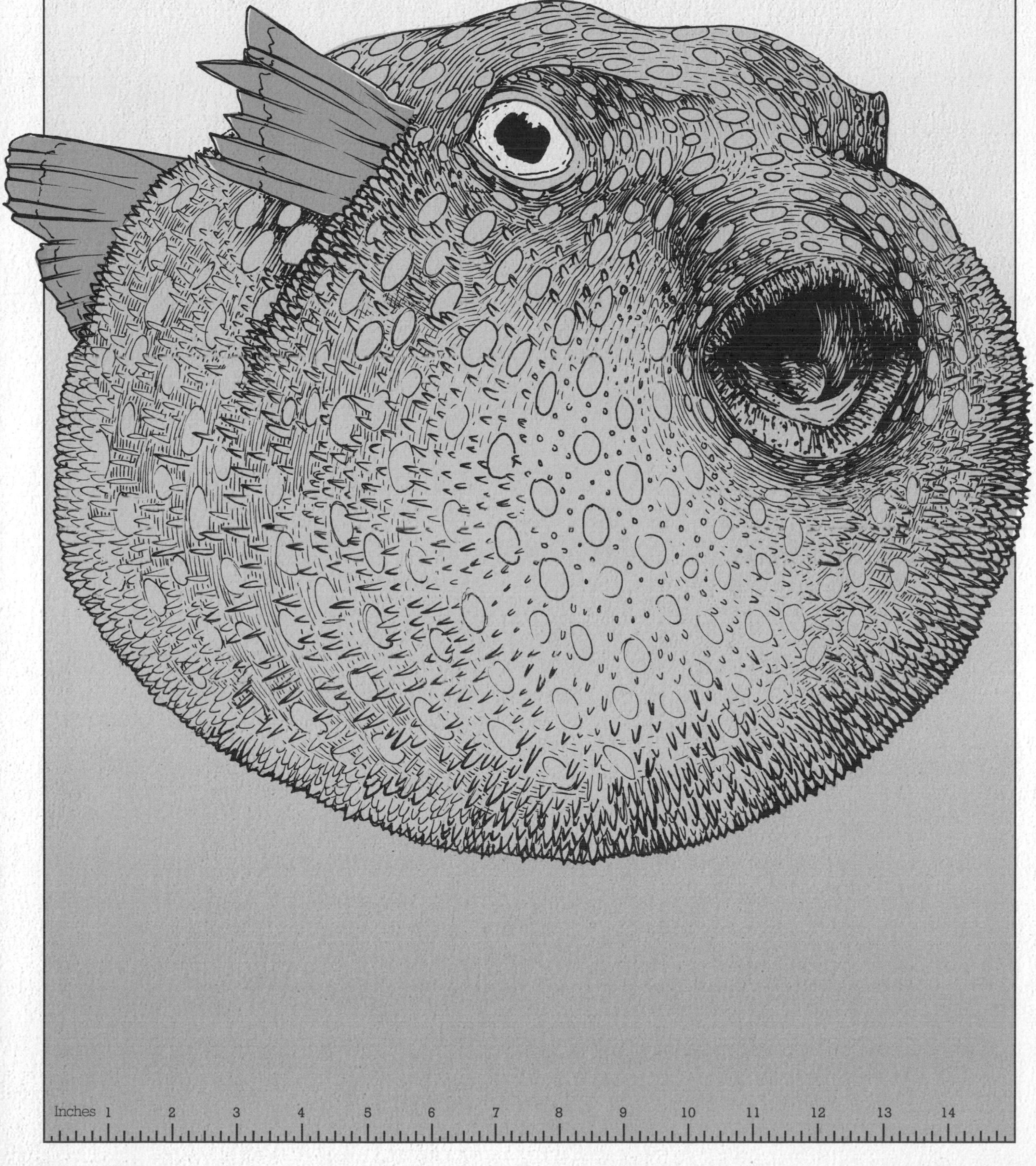

HAGFISH

KINGDOM	**Animalia**
PHYLUM	**Chordata**
CLASS	**Myxini**
ORDER	**Myxiniformes**
FAMILY	**Myxinidae**
GENUS	**Various**
SPECIES	**Various**

SCIENTIFIC NAME: **EPTATRETUS STOUTII (AND OTHERS)**

Found along ocean floors just about everywhere on the planet, this eellike fish (though it is not an eel) has the unusual capability of producing slime. Lots of slime! It uses this as a defense mechanism: when provoked, the hagfish secretes a sticky slime from glands along its body. Once the slime mixes with seawater, it quickly expands into even more slime. Soon, the hagfish is surrounded by this thick goo, which acts as a protective shield, and can even suffocate predators by clogging their gills. How does the hagfish escape its own slime? Well, it ties itself in a knot near its head, and then passes the knot down the length of its body to wipe the slime away.

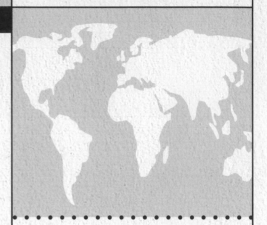

Distribution: In temperate regions just about everywhere on the planet . . . except the Red Sea.

Did you know?

Scientists and popular media often refer to the hagfish as the most disgusting of all sea creatures.

TOP 7 UNUSUAL HAGFISH NOTES

1 Hagfish are the only living animal to have a skull but no spine.

2 Hagfish have four hearts.

3 When their nostrils clog with their own slime, hagfish sneeze.

4 Hagfish are almost blind, but have well-developed senses of touch and smell.

5 Hagfish can change from male to female and female to male, depending on the season.

6 Hagfish can produce enough slime in a few minutes to fill five 1-gallon milk jugs.

7 Hagfish slime, different from other slimes, is full of tiny fibers, which makes it especially sticky and difficult to remove.

Fig. 38 Hagfish mouth.

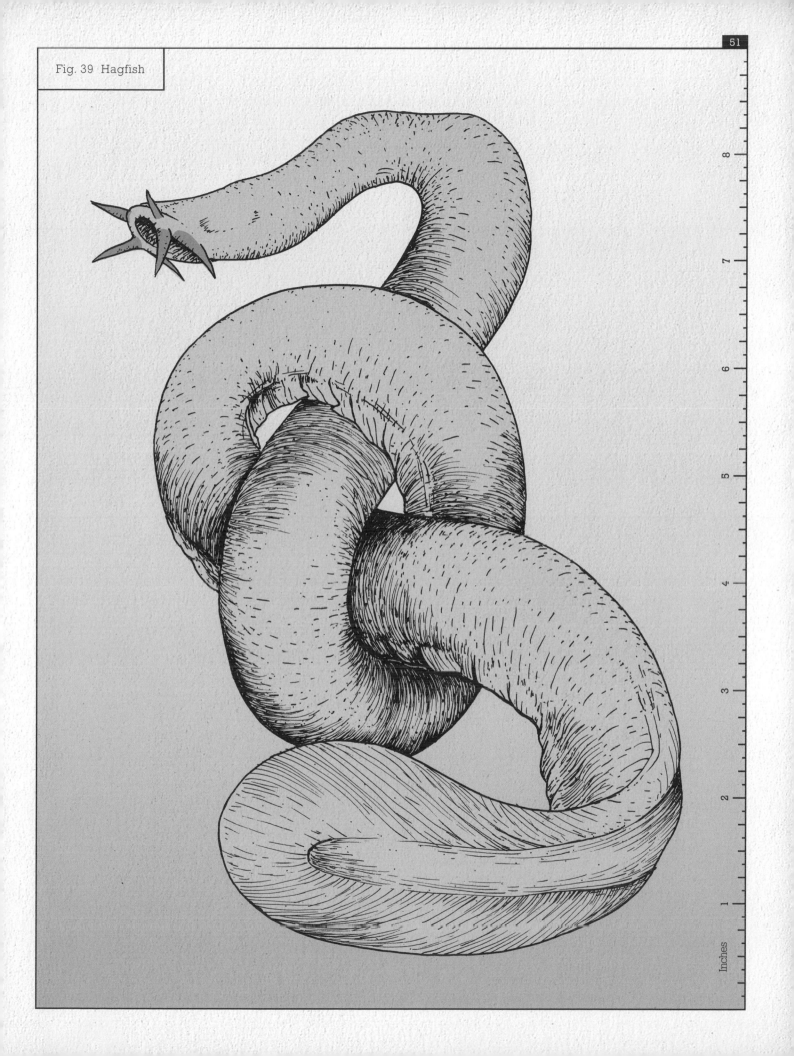

Fig. 39 Hagfish

HAMMER-HEADED BAT

SCIENTIFIC NAME: **HYPSIGNATHUS MONSTROSUS**

Welcome to the African rain forest, where one might find (or hear) the hammer-headed bat. With its enormous, moose-shaped noggin, the male hammer-headed bat can create a honk that rivals the loudest and most repetitive car alarms. Also known as the big-lipped bat, this animal is designed to make noise. Its larynx takes up more than half its body, its head is basically a giant resonating chamber, and its jumbo lips help project the sound even farther. The purpose for all this, of course, is to find a mate. When the female gets closer, the male will change his call into a rapid buzzing sound. And if she likes what she hears, the two are a match. After spending some quality time together, the female will push off into the air and respond with her own special farewell blast. HONNNNNK!

KINGDOM	**Animalia**
PHYLUM	**Chordata**
CLASS	**Mammalia**
ORDER	**Chiroptera**
FAMILY	**Pteropodidae**
GENUS	**Hypsignathus**
SPECIES	**H. monstrosus**

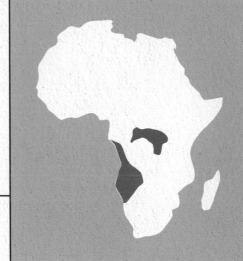

Distribution:
Central and western Africa.

TRUE OR FALSE?

1   The hammer-headed bat is the largest bat in Africa, with a wingspan that can reach up to 3 feet.

2   Hammer-headed bats are closely related to hammer-headed sharks. Both animals take pride in their ability to easily remove old, rusty nails from lumber.

3   The hammer-headed bat is a member of the suborder Megachiroptera, and it is also referred to as the megabat, the fruit bat, or the flying fox.

4   Hammer-headed bats are frugivores, which means they eat mostly fruit.

5   If a human is bitten by a hammer-headed bat, the human's head is likely to transform into a moose-like shape, and will thereafter be capable of making car-alarm sounds.

Answers: 1. T. 2. F. 3. T. 4. T. 5. F (But I would suggest you seek immediate medical attention.)

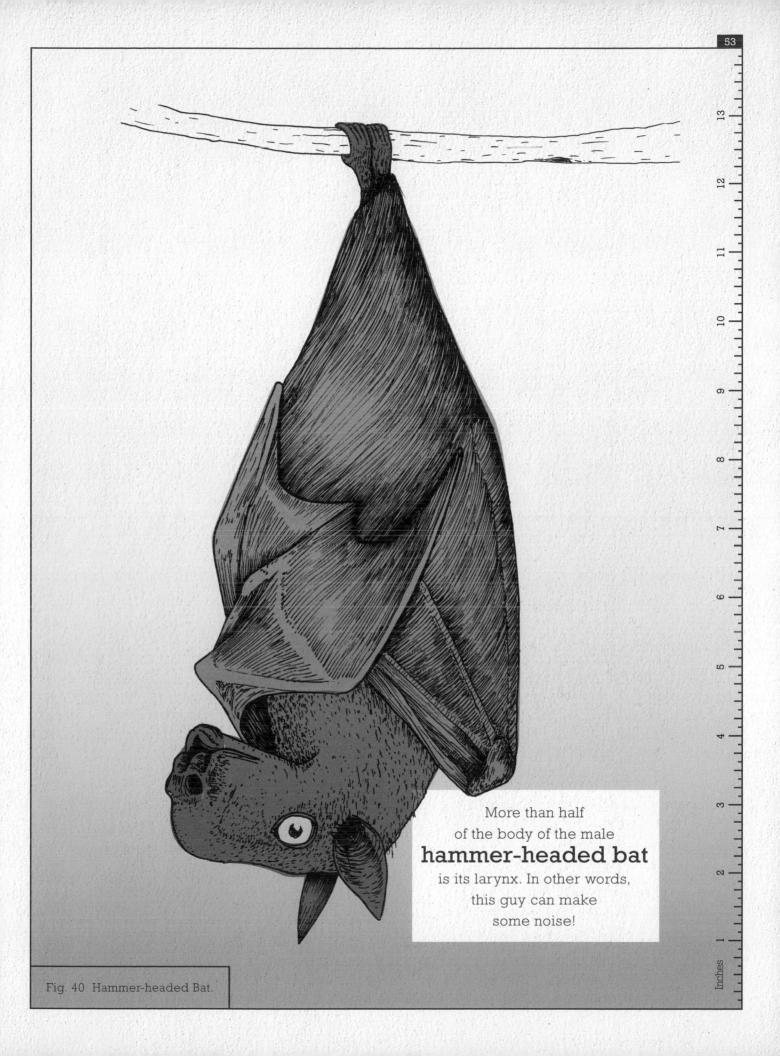

More than half
of the body of the male
hammer-headed bat
is its larynx. In other words,
this guy can make
some noise!

Fig. 40 Hammer-headed Bat.

KINGDOM	**Animalia**
PHYLUM	**Chordata**
CLASS	**Mammalia**
ORDER	**Carnivora**
FAMILY	**Mustelidae**
GENUS	**Mellivora**
SPECIES	**M. capensis**

HONEY

Distribution:
Central and southern
Africa, Saudi Arabia,
and India.

SCIENTIFIC NAME: MELLIVORA CAPENSIS

According to the 2002 edition of *Guinness World Records*, honey badgers are the "most fearless animal in the world." I'm not exactly sure how they determined that. I might have voted for the tardigrade, or perhaps Tony Hawk, for that matter. Nonetheless, this animal has quite an appetite, and will go after just about anything that crosses its path, no matter how dangerous. Named for its craving for honey, this badger is willing to break into beehives despite being stung numerous times during the process. And when it's done snacking on honey, it will continue hunting for rodents, birds, eggs, insects, lizards, tortoises, frogs, and even venomous snakes.

FEARLESS FACTORS

1 Honey badgers are also excellent climbers and can easily climb to the tops of trees, where they can attack bird nests and beehives.

2 The honey badger has been known to pull apart wooden boards and even dig under stone foundations to get at livestock. One incident in Kenya reports a sole honey badger killing 17 ducks and 36 chickens inside a single henhouse.

3 The skin on the honey badger is incredibly tough—enough so that it can resist dog bites, arrows, spears, and even machete blows from angry farmers.

4 Animal conservationists have very little concern for this animal due to its ability to easily adapt to just about any environment . . . and eat just about anything it feels like eating.

In. 1 2 3 4 5 6 7 8 9 10 11 12 13 14 15 16 17 18 19 20

BADGER

Fig. 41 Honey Badger

Fig. 42 Honey badger showing its teeth.

24 25 26 27 28 29 30 31 32 33 34 35 36 37 38 39 40 41 42 43

HORNED PUFFIN

SCIENTIFIC NAME: FRATERCULA CORNICULATA

As the name suggests, the horned puffin has small, fleshy black horns above its eyes. The horns are not stiff like a ram's horn (or like a trumpet, for that matter). Instead, they're soft epidermal papilla (growths from the skin) full of living tissue. The horned puffin is a sea bird and, typically, the only time it returns to shore is to breed in the spring. Horned puffins dive for their food, and live on a diet of fish, squid, and crustaceans. These birds are at risk from habitat loss, due to climate change and the introduction of rats (which eat the puffin eggs) onto some islands the birds use for nesting.

KINGDOM	**Animalia**
PHYLUM	**Chordata**
CLASS	**Aves**
ORDER	**Charadriiformes**
FAMILY	**Alcidae**
GENUS	Fratercula
SPECIES	**F. corniculata**

A HORNED PUFFIN POEM JUST FOR YOU!

The horned puffin is an awkward auk,
an avian of the sea.
It only travels to the shore in hopes it will agree
with another of its kind, so it can procreate.
It boasts a red and yellow bill, and a horn above its eye.
It even wears a tidy tux, with the exception of a tie.
Its clumsy feet are not so neat as it walks across the land,
but the good news is that in open sea
they lend a helping hand.

Distribution: North Pacific, with most of the population found along the coast of Siberia and from Alaska to Oregon.

Fig. 43 Horned puffin flying.

Did you know?

Horned puffins are camouflaged from predators both above and below! When they swim, underwater predators have a hard time seeing them because their white underbelly looks like the bright surface of the water. At the same time, they are also hard to spot from above because their dark-colored backs look like the dark ocean depths.

Fig. 44 Horned Puffin

Because of its colorful bill, the **horned puffin** is sometimes called the sea parrot.

HUMPBACK ANGLERFISH

KINGDOM	**Animalia**
PHYLUM	**Chordata**
CLASS	**Actinopterygii**
ORDER	**Lophiiformes**
FAMILY	**Melanocetidae**
GENUS	**Melanocetus**
SPECIES	**M. johnsonii**

SCIENTIFIC NAME: MELANOCETUS JOHNSONII

Indeed, the humpback anglerfish is one of the ocean's strangest-looking deep-sea creatures. These bony fish are named for the fleshy growth on their heads, which acts as a bioluminescent lure to attract their prey. This fish is found worldwide in near-freezing water at depths of up to 6,000 feet below the water surface. Other notable features include an enormous mouth full of some seriously long and sharp teeth.

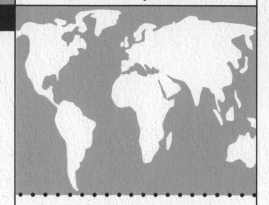

Distribution: Oceans worldwide.

THE HUMPBACK ANGLERFISH: A SHORT POEM

The humpback anglerfish fishes for fish
like we humans do.
However, its fishing pole is attached to its head.
It waits to catch a few.
Its sharp and pointy teeth are ready
for the big surprise.
Good thing its bones can flex,
for it can eat things twice its own size.

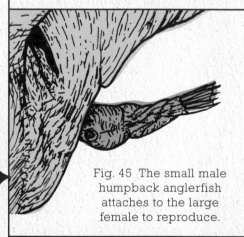

Fig. 45 The small male humpback anglerfish attaches to the large female to reproduce.

Did you know?

As if it's not bizarre enough that the humpback anglerfish carries a lantern on its head, the way it reproduces is even stranger! The smaller male bites down on the female and releases an enzyme that causes him to fuse into her skin. He disintegrates into her body, becoming nothing more than a lump. This lump stays attached, ready to fertilize her eggs when the time comes.

POP QUIZ

Thanks to their headlamps, anglerfish also make excellent:

A   theater ushers.
B   coal miners.
C   ghost hunters.
D   night-duty security guards.

Answer: None of the above.

BITE ▸ FUSE ▸ DISINTEGRATE ▸ PROCREATE!

Fig. 46 Humpback Anglerfish

Bioluminsecent
lantern.

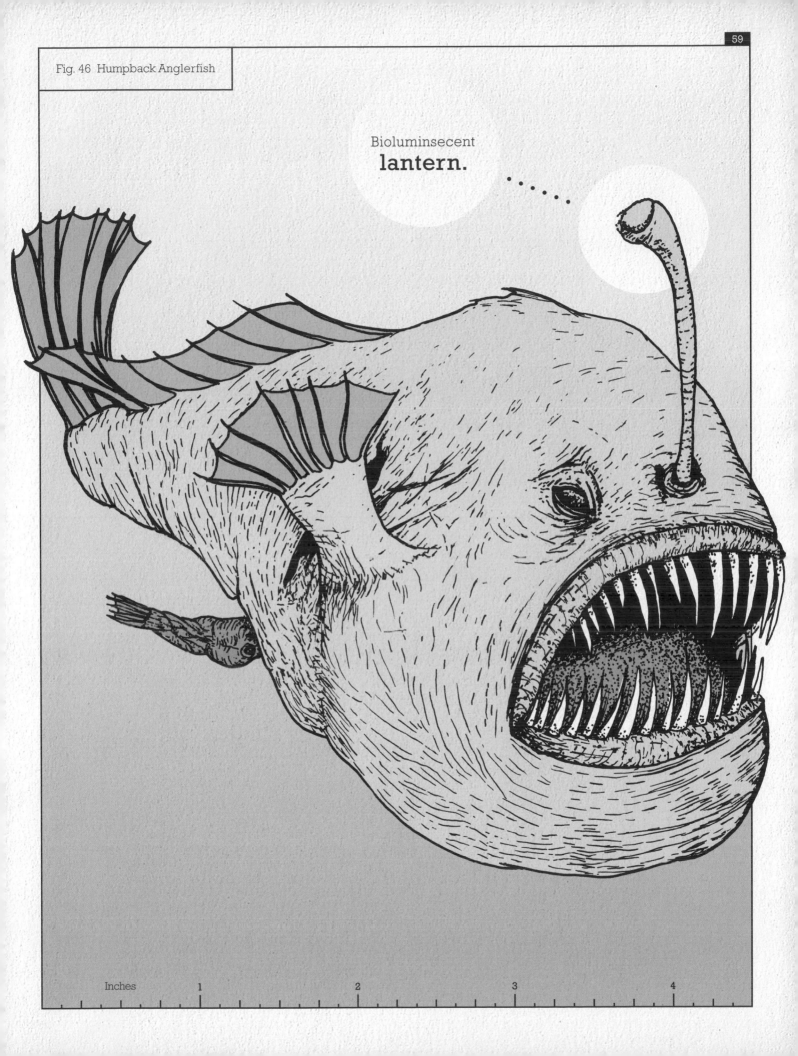

Inches   1   2   3   4

JESUS CHRIST LIZARD

SCIENTIFIC NAME: BASILISCUS BASILISCUS

Behold the Jesus Christ lizard! People have given the common basilisk this name because of its amazing ability to run on water. Found in the tropical rain forests, this lizard has scaly fringes on its feet. When it senses danger, it can open these fringes, which increase the surface area of its feet and allows it to run across water without sinking. The adult basilisk can travel over water for distances of 15 feet. The younger and thus lighter basilisk can run as far as 30 to 60 feet.

KINGDOM	**Animalia**
PHYLUM	**Chordata**
CLASS	**Reptilia**
ORDER	**Squamata**
FAMILY	**Corytophanidae**
GENUS	**Basiliscus**
SPECIES	**B. basiliscus**

Fig. 47 Jesus Christ Lizard

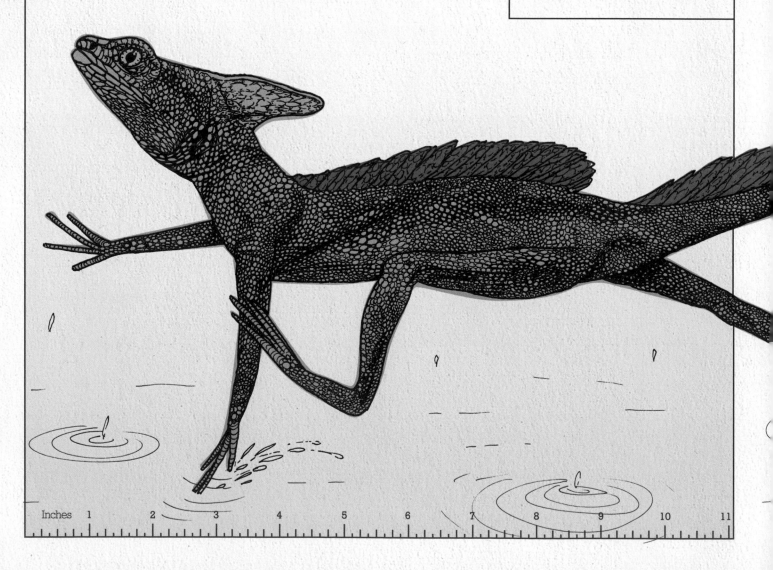

Inches 1 2 3 4 5 6 7 8 9 10 11

TRUE OR FALSE?

1 The basilisk in Greek mythology is a combination of a rooster, snake, and lion, and can turn a man to stone with its gaze.

2 The Jesus Christ lizard has similar abilities, but its predators turn into motorized Christmas lawn ornaments.

3 The Jesus Christ lizard is also an excellent swimmer and is capable of holding its breath for up to 30 minutes.

4 The female basilisk will lay up to 20 eggs, and then leave them to hatch on their own. The hatchlings are born with the ability to run on water.

5 Newborn basilisks are referred to as Baby Jesus lizards.

Answers: 1. T. 2. F. 3. T. 4. T. 5. F. (Well, that's what I would call them.)

Distribution: Central America and parts of Colombia and Venezuela.

60 feet

Fig. 48 This is how the Jesus Christ lizard runs over water.

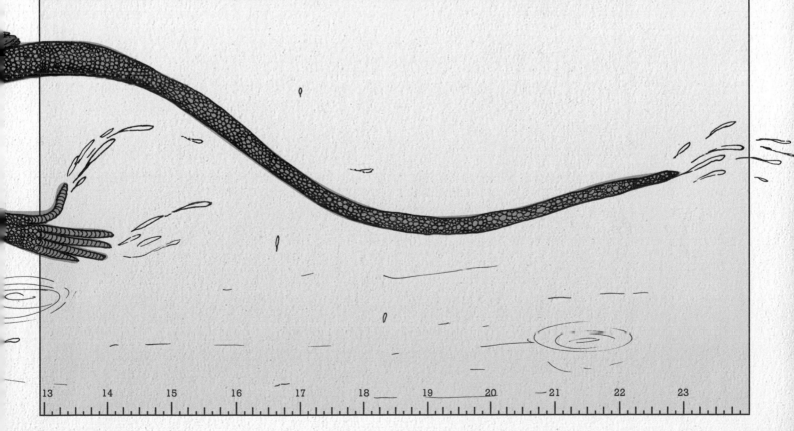

13   14   15   16   17   18   19   20   21   22   23

KOMODO DRAGON

SCIENTIFIC NAME: **VARANUS KOMODOENSIS**

Reaching 10 feet in length and weighing as much as 300 pounds, Komodo dragons are the largest living lizards on the planet. These reptiles can be found on the island of Komodo as well as on three other Indonesian islands. With its long, flat head, scaly skin, huge, muscular tail, bowed legs, and long claws, this dragon rules its domain. It eats just about anything and every-thing: birds, pigs, goats, deer, buffalo, horses, and even smaller Komodo dragons. If, by chance, its prey happens to be lucky enough to escape the dragon's jaws after being bitten, it is likely to keel over dead in the next 24 hours thanks to the reptile's deadly venom. In addition, the Komodo dragons' saliva contains at least 57 different strains of bacteria. Dragon breath, anyone?

KINGDOM	**Animalia**
PHYLUM	**Chordata**
CLASS	**Reptilia**
ORDER	**Squamata**
FAMILY	**Varanidae**
GENUS	**Varanus**
SPECIES	**V. komodoensis**

Did you know?

Although the Komodo dragon has been around for millions of years, their existence was unknown to the Western world until about 100 years ago.

There have been at least a dozen documented cases of humans killed by Komodo dragons in the past 20 years.

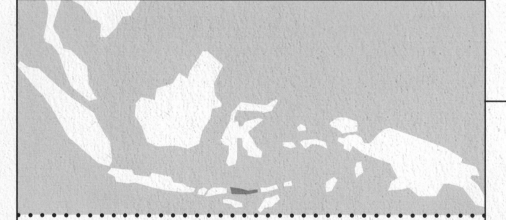

Distribution:
Indonesia's Lesser Sunda Islands.

Most of the people who live on the island of Komodo are descendants of former convicts who were exiled to the island. However, I don't think this has anything to do with Komodo dragons. Then again, maybe it does?

Did you know?

Fig. 49 Komodo Dragon

Komodo dragons
spend most of their youth in
trees and descend to the ground
only when they are large enough
to avoid being eaten by
larger dragons.

Feet   1   2   3

LEAFY SEA DRAGON

SCIENTIFIC NAME: PHYCODURUS EQUES

Perfectly camouflaged among the kelp and algae, the leafy sea dragon can be found along the southern and western coasts of Australia. It delicately floats next to reefs, easily blending in with its surroundings. Of course, this helps keep the leafy sea dragon safe from its numerous predators. Related to seahorses (and even more closely to the weedy sea dragon), the leafy sea dragon—with its long leaf-like skin growths—is by far the most elaborate-looking fish in the family. And despite its small size, this creature is a carnivore. The leafy sea dragon uses its pipe-like snout to suck plankton and even small shrimp and fish into its toothless mouth.

KINGDOM	**Animalia**
PHYLUM	**Chordata**
CLASS	**Actinopterygii**
ORDER	**Syngnathiformes**
FAMILY	**Syngnathidae**
GENUS	**Phycodurus**
SPECIES	**P. eques**

Distribution: The waters of Australia from Kangaroo Island on the southern shoreline to Jurien Bay on the western shoreline.

It's the male leafy sea dragon that cares for the eggs. After the female deposits 200-plus eggs onto the male's tail, the male leafy sea dragon carries them around for the next 9 weeks. While the father is tending to the birth of the miniature sea dragons, perhaps the mother is off smoking a cigar?

Did you know?

Fig. 50 Leafy sea dragon carrying eggs.

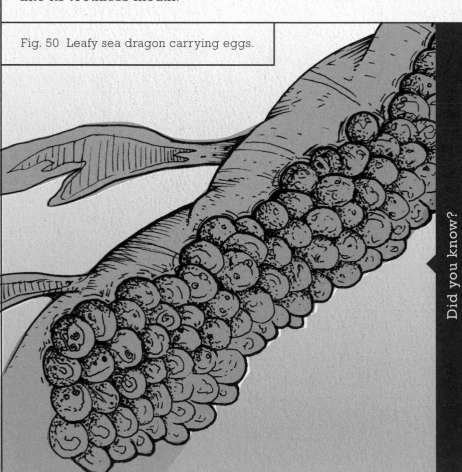

The **leafy sea dragon** has protrusions all over its body that look like floating seaweed.

Fig. 51 Leafy Sea Dragon

13
12
11
10
9
8
7
6
5
4
3
2
1
Inches

LONG-EARED JERBOA

SCIENTIFIC NAME: **EUCHOREUTES NASO**

Indeed it looks like a kangaroo (or some sort of hopping marsupial), but it's, in fact, a small nocturnal rodent. The long-eared jerboa is found in the deserts of China and Mongolia, where it spends most of the day burrowed under the sand. At night, it ventures out, hopping around in search of insects to eat. The long-eared jerboa's body length is only about 3 inches, plus 6 more inches of tail, which it uses to help prop itself upright. As the name suggests, this unusual creature has a set of extraordinarily large ears, which no doubt help it listen for predators. The long-eared jerboa is thought to hibernate throughout the winter months, and breed soon thereafter. They probably produce 2 litters (each containing 2 to 6 little jerboas) during the summer months. Other than that, very little is known about this specific species of jerboa, other than the fact that it is endangered. At the time of writing this book, there were only two video clips of the long-eared jerboa on YouTube.

KINGDOM	**Animalia**
PHYLUM	**Chordata**
CLASS	**Mammalia**
ORDER	**Rodentia**
FAMILY	**Dipodidae**
GENUS	**Euchoreutes**
SPECIES	**E. naso**

Distribution:
Mongolia and China.

Did you know?

The long-eared jerboa's ears are two-thirds the size of its body. If this were the case for humans, adults would have ears over 3 feet long!

Fig. 52

There are about 30 different species of jerboa on the planet (most of them living in Asia), including the lesser Egyptian jerboa, the five-toed pygmy jerboa, and the thick-tailed three-toed jerboa.

Fig. 53 Long-eared Jerboa

Inches   1   2   3

MAGNAPINNA SQUID

SCIENTIFIC NAME: **MAGNAPINNA ATLANTICA (AND OTHERS)**

The Magnapinna squid is a deep-sea squid that was first sighted in 1988. This particular cephalopod looks very different from all previously known squids—the appendages of the Magnapinna squid extend sideways from the body, and then bend down, giving the appearance of dangling elbows. Most remarkable is the length of the elastic tentacles, which have been estimated to stretch up to 15 to 20 times the length of the body, giving the squid a total span of more than 26 feet.

4,000 feet

Fig. 54

KINGDOM	**Animalia**
PHYLUM	**Mollusca**
CLASS	**Cephalopoda**
ORDER	**Teuthida**
FAMILY	**Magnapinnidae**
GENUS	**Magnapinna**
SPECIES	**Various**

Distribution:
Indian Ocean, north of Hawaii, off the northern coast of Brazil, and the Gulf of Mexico.

THE MAGNAPINNA SQUID: A SHORT POEM

The Magnapinna squid was discovered very late.
The first documented sighting was in 1988.
The reason for this, as you can imagine,
is as simple as can be:
It lives at a depth of 4,000 feet below the surface of the sea.
But until we have an easier way to reach the deepest deep-sea zones,
with this cephalopod, we're in the dark.
Very little yet is known . . .

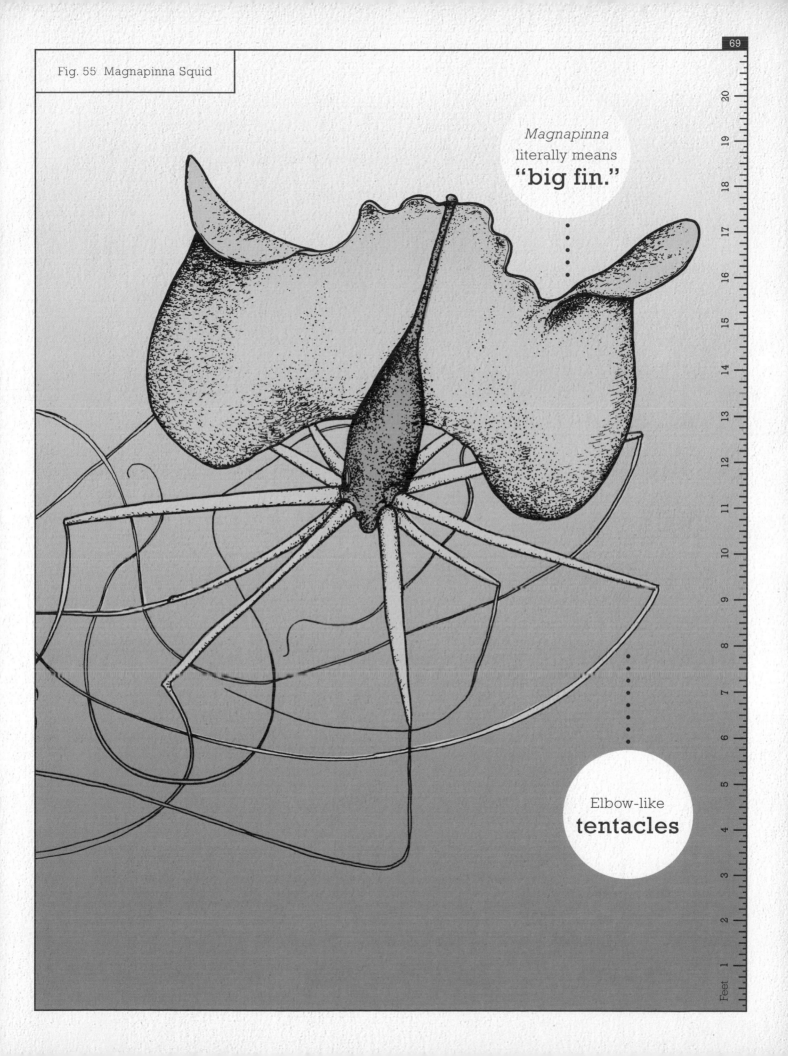

Fig. 55 Magnapinna Squid

Magnapinna
literally means
"big fin."

Elbow-like
tentacles

Feet

MIMIC OCTOPUS

SCIENTIFIC NAME: **THAUMOCTOPUS MIMICUS**

The mimic octopus can mimic other animals! It does this to help avoid predators (though it might also do it from time to time just for fun. I certainly would if I were a mimic octopus). Amazingly, this clever octopus was not discovered until 1998. All octopuses can change the color and texture of their skin to blend in with rocks, algae, and coral, but this is the first octopus discovered that can shape itself to look like other animals. The mimic octopus is approximately 2 feet long and slithers along the muddy seafloor, where it feasts on shrimp, snails, and various small fish. It has been observed to mimic the shape of sea snakes, giant crabs, flounders, sea anemones, mantis shrimp, and stingrays.

KINGDOM	**Animalia**
PHYLUM	**Mollusca**
CLASS	**Cephalopoda**
ORDER	**Octopoda**
FAMILY	**Octopodidae**
GENUS	**Thaumoctopus**
SPECIES	**T. mimicus**

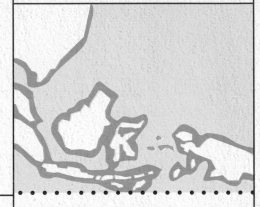

Distribution: The coast of Indonesia and Malaysia.

Fig. 56
The many faces of
the mimic octopus.

TWO VERY IMPORTANT FACTS ABOUT THE MIMIC OCTOPUS

1. According to *The American Heritage Dictionary*, the plural form of octopus is either octopuses or octopi. (For example, look at all the mimic octopuses!)

2. If you play charades with a mimic octopus, the octopus will win.

Sole fish · · · · · · · · · · · · · · · · · Lionfish · · · · · · · · · · · · · · · · · Sea snake

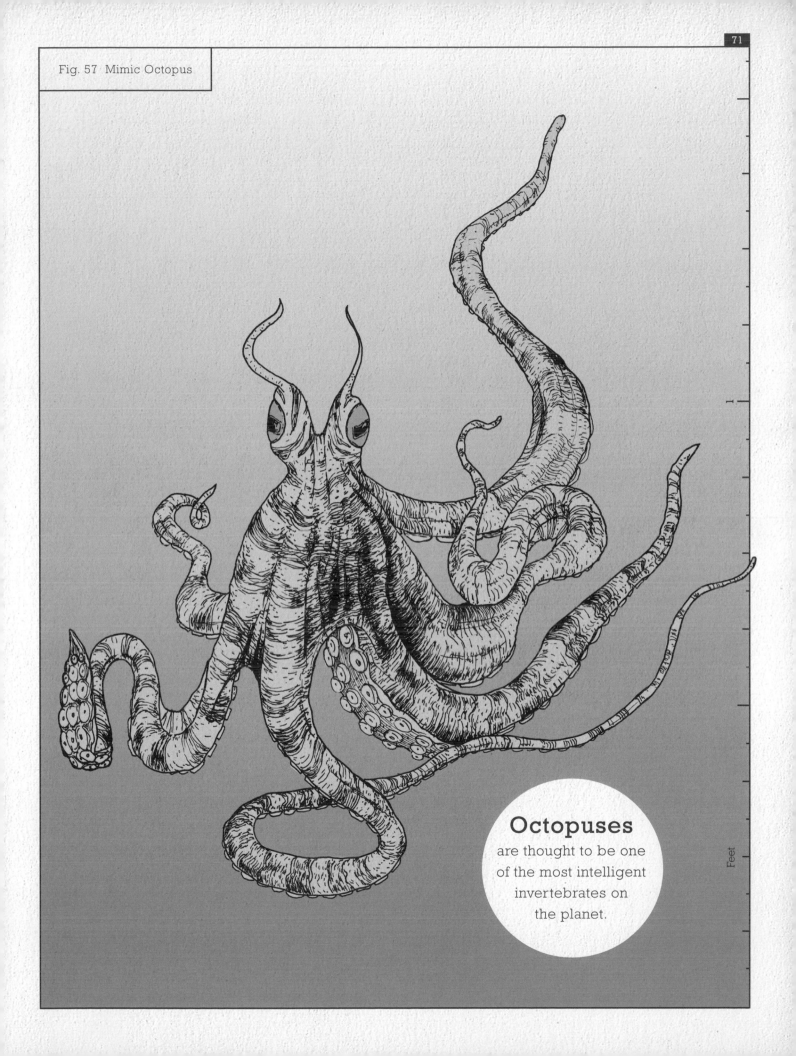

Fig. 57 Mimic Octopus

Feet

Octopuses are thought to be one of the most intelligent invertebrates on the planet.

NARWHAL

SCIENTIFIC NAME: **MONODON MONOCEROS**

KINGDOM	**Animalia**
PHYLUM	**Chordata**
CLASS	**Mammalia**
ORDER	**Cetacea**
FAMILY	**Monodontidae**
GENUS	**Monodon**
SPECIES	**M. monoceros**

Unicorn of the sea! The narwhal is a midsize whale that lives year-round in the Arctic Ocean. The male narwhal features a long, swordlike tusk extending from his upper jaw. Why from his jaw? Because it's actually a tooth! The tooth is helical (spiral shaped), and can grow up to 9 feet in length. Scientists are not quite certain why the male narwhal has this tusk, but it is assumed that it is used to impress females or to battle rival suitors. Females sometimes grow a small tusk of their own, but it is not nearly as prominent as that of the male.

LEGEND OF THE HORN

Some historians believe that ancient Vikings hunted the narwhal while out at sea, and then brought the tusks back and sold them to traders. The traders, in turn, sold the tusks as unicorn horns to gullible people who believed that they were an antidote to poison. Of course, nobody has ever actually seen a unicorn . . . unless you happened to go to the Ringling Bros. circus in 1985 as I did. By the way, why is it called a *unicorn* anyway, and not a *unihorn*?

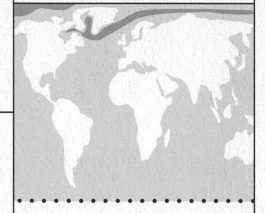

Distribution:
Atlantic and Russian areas of the Arctic Ocean.

Did you know?

Narwhal means "corpse whale" in Old Norse. This, most likely, is a description of the whale's skin, which is bluish-gray with white blotches . . . sort of like a rotting corpse.

Did you know?

The narwhal typically hangs out in groups of 4 to 20, known as a pod, and can live up to 50 years.

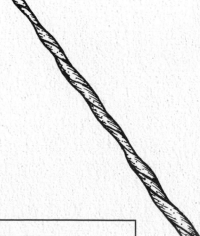

Fig. 58 Narwhal tusk

Fig. 59 Narwhal

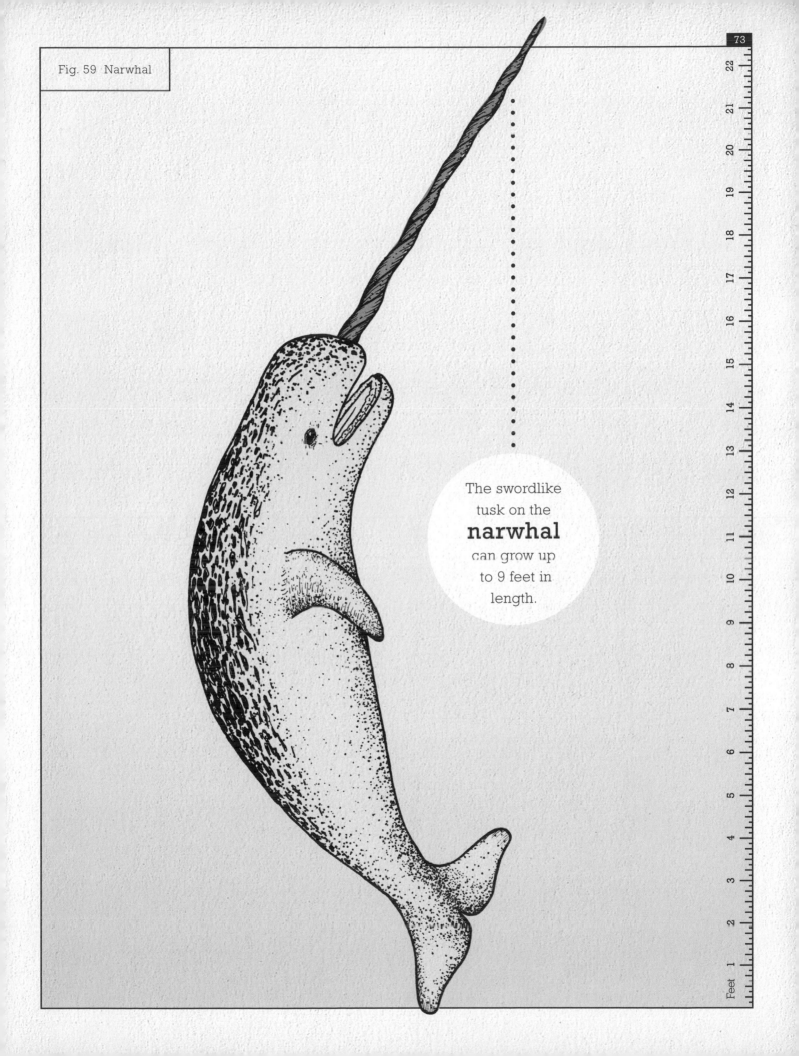

The swordlike tusk on the **narwhal** can grow up to 9 feet in length.

Feet 1 2 3 4 5 6 7 8 9 10 11 12 13 14 15 16 17 18 19 20 21 22

OLM

SCIENTIFIC NAME: **PROTEUS ANGUINUS**

Also known as the proteus, the olm is a blind amphibian found only in the underwater caves of southern Europe, specifically parts of Italy, Croatia, and Slovenia. Its snakelike body is covered with very thin skin with very little pigment, which renders the salamander white or pink in color. And because it lives its entire life in darkness, the olm's eyes are undeveloped, causing the creature to be blind. What it does have, however, are incredible senses of smell and hearing, as well as ampulary organs, which can detect electrical fields. This helps the olm find both its way through the darkness as well as its prey, which includes small crabs and snails. Food, however, is not so crucial considering the olm can live up to 10 years without eating.

KINGDOM	**Animalia**
PHYLUM	**Chordata**
CLASS	**Amphibia**
ORDER	**Caudata**
FAMILY	**Proteidae**
GENUS	**Proteus**
SPECIES	**P. anguinus**

Fig. 60 Olm

Distribution:
Italy, southern Slovenia, southwestern Croatia, and Herzegovina.

The **olm** is a symbol of Slovenian natural heritage, and was depicted on the 10 stotinov coin. This was basically their penny before the euro took over in 2007.

Did you know?

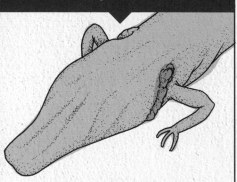

Fig. 61 The olm's eyes are undeveloped. This creature is blind!

Inches

PEA FROG

SCIENTIFIC NAME: MICROHYLA NEPENTHICOLA

The pea frog is the smallest frog outside of North and South America (making it the second smallest frog in the world) . . . at least, that is, until a smaller frog is discovered. Considering this minuscule creature was only formally announced in 2010, there's no telling what scientists will find next. The pea frog was actually documented for more than 100 years, but it was assumed to be the juvenile of another frog species. Researchers then realized that the tiny hoppers were, in fact, full-grown adults. This revelation was made after hearing the frog's mating call . . . which is only made by adult frogs. The pea frog spends most of its time hanging out in the mouth of pitcher plants. These plants have oval openings and grow in the damp, dark forests of Borneo. The frog deposits its eggs onto the sides of the pitcher, and tadpoles grow in the liquid that accumulates inside the plant. The pea frog's tadpoles measure just 0.12 inch long.

KINGDOM	**Animalia**
PHYLUM	**Chordata**
CLASS	**Amphibia**
ORDER	**Anura**
FAMILY	**Microhylidae**
GENUS	**Microhyla**
SPECIES	**M. nepenthicola**

Distribution: Sarawak, Borneo.

Fig. 62 Pea Frog

What is the difference between toads and frogs? Toads are frogs! However, toads are typically rounder, drier, and wartier.

Fig. 63

Pea Frog
0.5 inch

Gray Tree Frog
2 inches

Glass Frog
2.8 inches

Bullfrog
6 inches

Goliath Frog
12 inches

Inches

KINGDOM	**Animalia**
PHYLUM	**Chordata**
CLASS	**Mammalia**
ORDER	**Cingulata**
FAMILY	**Dasypodidae**
GENUS	**Chlamyphorus**
SPECIES	**C. truncatus**

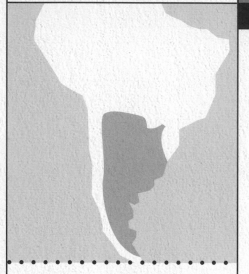

Distribution: Argentina.

PINK

SCIENTIFIC NAME: **CHLAMYPHORUS TRUNCATUS**

There are about 20 species of armadillo, but the pink fairy is the smallest (about 5 inches), and certainly the most fashionable. Looking somewhat like a hamster hiding in a lobster shell, this little creature roams the dry, sandy plains of central Argentina, where it snacks mostly on ants, worms, and a few plants. Thanks to a set of large (well, relatively) front claws and its torpedo-shaped head, it has the amazing ability to completely bury itself underground in a matter of seconds. In fact, it can move through the sand so quickly that it appears to swim. Its body armor protects it from getting scratched up by the sand during the process. Like so many other creatures in this book, due to habitat destruction, the pink fairy armadillo may now be a threatened species.

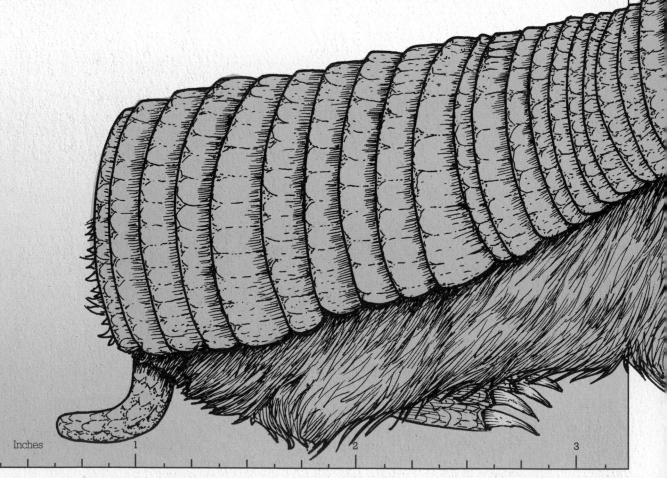

Inches	1	2	3

FAIRY ARMADILLO

TRUE OR FALSE?

Fig. 64 Pink Fairy Armadillo

1 Baby armadillos have soft shells, which don't completely harden until they are fully grown.

2 The pink fairy armadillo lives underground and is nocturnal.

3 Pink fairy armadillos keep small pink magic wands under their shells, which they use on special occasions.

4 Armadillos are distantly related to anteaters and sloths.

5 To escape predators, armadillos will curl up in a tight ball and roll away as fast as possible.

Answers: 1. T, 2. T, 3. F, 4. T, 5. F (With the exception of the three-banded armadillo, which can curl into a ball to elude predators. Of course, it won't roll away . . . unless it happens to be on a hill.)

The word ***armadillo*** is Spanish for "small armed one."

4   5   6

PLATYPUS

SCIENTIFIC NAME: ORNITHORHYNCHUS ANATINUS

This semiaquatic mammal (which has traits associated with both birds and reptiles) can be found on the edges of rivers and lakes in eastern Australia. Along with the echidna, the platypus is one of only 5 living species of mammal that lay eggs instead of giving birth to live young. With its duck bill, beaver tail, and otter feet, early European settlers were seriously confused by this animal when they first arrived in Australia. Many even thought it was a hoax. Perhaps it is?

KINGDOM	Animalia
PHYLUM	Chordata
CLASS	Mammalia
ORDER	Monotremata
FAMILY	Ornithorhynchidae
GENUS	Ornithorhynchus
SPECIES	O. anatinus

Distribution: Eastern Australia and Tasmania.

The **platypus's** tail stores up to 50 percent of the animal's fat. This provides the platypus with an energy reserve in case food becomes scarce.

Inches 1 2 5 6 7 8

PLATYFACTS

1 The male platypus has a single sharp, hollow spur on each hind ankle. These spurs contain venom that can kill a small animal.

2 The platypus swims with its eyes, ears, and nose shut.

3 Like the echidna, the female platypus does not have nipples. Instead she secretes milk from two round patches of skin on her belly.

4 The platypus bill is rubbery and flexible. It is not recyclable.

5 The platypus is one of the only known mammals to have a sense of electroreception: the ability to perceive electrical impulses generated by other animals. This helps it find food.

Did you know?

Unlike the octopus, there is no agreed-upon plural form
of platypus, though scientists typically use "platypuses"
or "platypus." Not "platypi." Sorry.

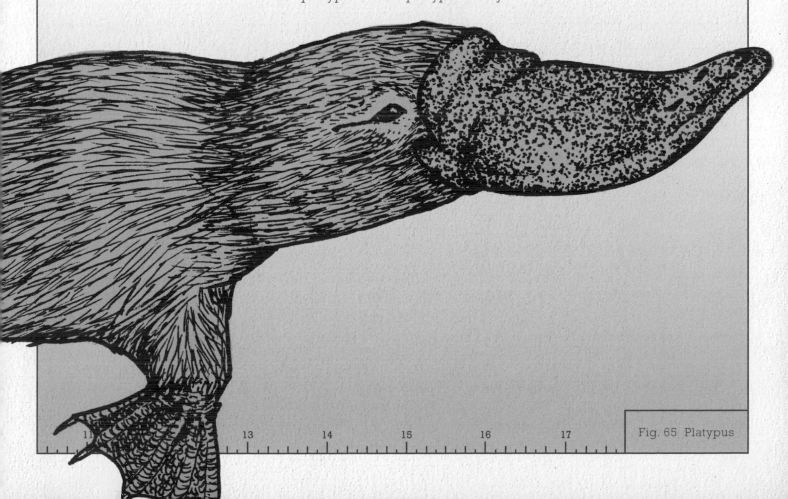

Fig. 65 Platypus

PYGMY MARMOSET

SCIENTIFIC NAME: CALLITHRIX PYGMAEA

Also known as the dwarf monkey, the pygmy marmoset is the smallest monkey on the planet, with a body length ranging from 5 to 6 inches, and a weight of about 4 ounces. These unusual creatures can be found in the rain forests of the upper Amazon, running and jumping among the trees and shrubs. Thanks to its low weight, the pygmy marmoset can reach the tops of trees (where larger moneys can't go) and gather fruits, berries, and insects. Most often, the pygmy marmoset can be found in groups of 2 to 6, consisting of the mother, father, and their offspring. Yay for the happy marmoset family!

KINGDOM	Animalia
PHYLUM	Chordata
CLASS	Mammalia
ORDER	Primates
FAMILY	Cebide
GENUS	Callithrix
SPECIES	C. pygmaea

Distribution: Peru, Ecuador, Colombia, Bolivia, and Brazil.

Pygmy marmoset monkeys communicate using high-pitched whistling sounds. Among their families, they also communicate through facial expressions and body language. Pygmy marmosets can produce an ultrasonic cry that is inaudible to humans. This is typically used to alert their family to danger.

Inches

1

2

3

4

Fig. 66 Baby Pygmy Marmoset

SADDLEBACK CATERPILLAR

SCIENTIFIC NAME: **SIBINE STIMULEA**

Also known as a packsaddle, this caterpillar has markings on its back that resemble a saddle. A green saddle! To boot, the saddleback caterpillar comes equipped with spiny stinging hairs. If a human is unfortunate enough to innocently brush against a saddleback caterpillar, the sting is likely to be very painful, and may cause swelling, nausea, and even a long-lasting rash.

KINGDOM	**Animalia**
PHYLUM	**Arthropoda**
CLASS	**Insecta**
ORDER	**Lepidoptera**
FAMILY	**Limacodidae**
GENUS	**Sibine**
SPECIES	**S. stimulea**

A SADDLEBACK CATERPILLAR POEM JUST FOR YOU!

This fancy larval moth wears a saddle on its back.
And although it's rather pretty, beware, for it can attack.
Urticating hairs. Look out! Stay away!
For the sting can cause a rash,
which may last for many a day.

Distribution:
Texas to Florida, and north to Missouri and Massachusetts.

Did you know?

If you brush against a saddleback caterpillar, place a piece of Scotch Tape over the contact spot and remove it quickly—the hairs will stick to the tape. The sooner you do this, the less effect the sting will have.

Fig. 67 Saddleback Caterpillar

Inches 1

SEA PIG

KINGDOM	**Animalia**
PHYLUM	**Echinodermata**
CLASS	**Holothuroidea**
ORDER	**Elasipodida**
FAMILY	**Elpidiidae**
GENUS	**Scotoplanes**
SPECIES	**Various**

SCIENTIFIC NAME: **SCOTOPLANES GLOBOSA (AND OTHERS)**

Living in the deepest, darkest depths of the ocean's abyss are some rather unusual creatures known as sea pigs! The sea pig is part of a group of marine animals that includes sea squirts, sea slugs, corals, clams, sponges, and urchins. Needless to say, sea pigs earned their nickname because of their puffy legs and plump, pinkish appearance. The legs are arranged in a circular ring around the animal's bottom surface, and are used to push food into its mouths. And what look like antennae on the front of the head are also feet used to help propel the sea pig along the ocean floor. Sea pigs mostly feed on bits of decayed plants and animals found in the deep-sea mud. However, they especially like food that has recently fallen from the ocean's surface (such as a whale corpse). Sea pigs are often found in clusters of 300 or more, and each individual is just about the perfect size to fit in the palm of your hand. I would suggest that the sea pig might make an awesome pet, but you would first need to find a 3,000-foot-deep fishbowl.

Distribution: Deep ocean bottoms, specifically on the abyssal plain in the Atlantic, Pacific, and Indian Oceans, as well as off the Antarctic shelf.

Fig. 68 Sea Pig

Did you know?

Sea pigs are often found traveling together in large groups, all marching in the same direction. But where are they going?

Inches   1   2   3

SLOW LORIS

KINGDOM	Animalia
PHYLUM	Chordata
CLASS	Mammalia
ORDER	Primates
FAMILY	Lorisidae
GENUS	Nycticebus
SPECIES	Various

SCIENTIFIC NAME: NYCTICEBUS COUCANG (AND OTHERS)

The slow loris is a small nocturnal primate native to Southeast Asia. As the name implies, this creature is quite slooooow (though not as slow as the three-toed sloth). It moves deliberately from branch to branch while foraging for food. Slow lorises also have a very slow rate of metabolism, which allows them to digest things that most other animals can't, like tree sap. Many sources state that the slow loris is a venomous primate. This, however, is highly debatable. The "venom," which is a secretion from a gland in the slow loris's arm, contains an allergen equal in strength to that found in the saliva and sebaceous glands of domestic cats. In short, the slow loris has the ability to lick its arm, and then deliver a bite, which may or may not cause an allergic reaction in its victim. Either way, being bitten by a slow loris is something you want to avoid.

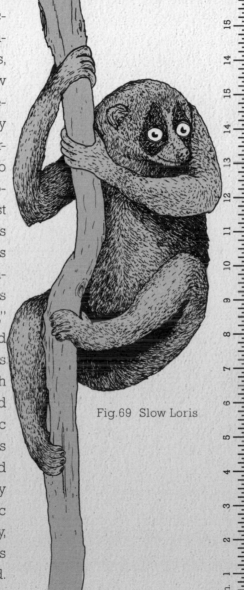

Fig.69 Slow Loris

Distribution:
Southern and Southeast Asia.

Did you know?

Some people believe that the
slow loris
possesses supernatural powers, such as the ability to ward off evil spirits and heal wounds. Unfortunately, people kill the slow loris for these supposed powers.

Although the slow loris is incredibly adorable, and has occasionally been sold as a pet, particularly in Japan (for as much as $4,000), owners soon discover that the slow loris is a wild animal that bites! Not to mention it's illegal. Don't do it!

Did you know?

SOLENODON

SCIENTIFIC NAME: **SOLENODON PARADOXUS & CUBANUS**

KINGDOM	**Animalia**
PHYLUM	**Chordata**
CLASS	**Mammalia**
ORDER	**Soricomorpha**
FAMILY	**Solenodontidae**
GENUS	**Solenodon**
SPECIES	**S. paradoxus, S. cubanus**

One of the most unusual (and, unfortunately, most threatened) mammals on the planet is the solenodon. The ancestors of these ancient creatures managed to survive the asteroid that wiped out the dinosaurs, major changes to Earth's climate, and even the biggest threat of all—the arrival of humans. Although the solenodon once lived all over North America, it is now found only on the islands of Cuba and Hispaniola. With its long, flexible snout, the solenodon can sniff around holes and crevices where insects, worms, and other invertebrates might be hiding. And then, with a deadly, venomous bite, the solenodon quickly incapacitates its prey, and dinner is ready.

Distribution: Hispaniola (Haiti and the Dominican Republic) and Cuba.

Did you know?

Solenodons are incredibly clumsy runners. When alarmed and trying to run quickly, they will often trip over their own feet and even tumble head-over-heels.

Solenodon, solenodon–
since dinosaurs, you've carried on.
But now it seems you're almost gone.
solenodon, solenodon.

Solenodon, solenodon–
your venomous bite will keep you strong.
We praise your courage and your brawn,
solenodon, solenodon.

THE SOLENODON: A SHORT POEM

Fig. 70 Solenodon tripping.

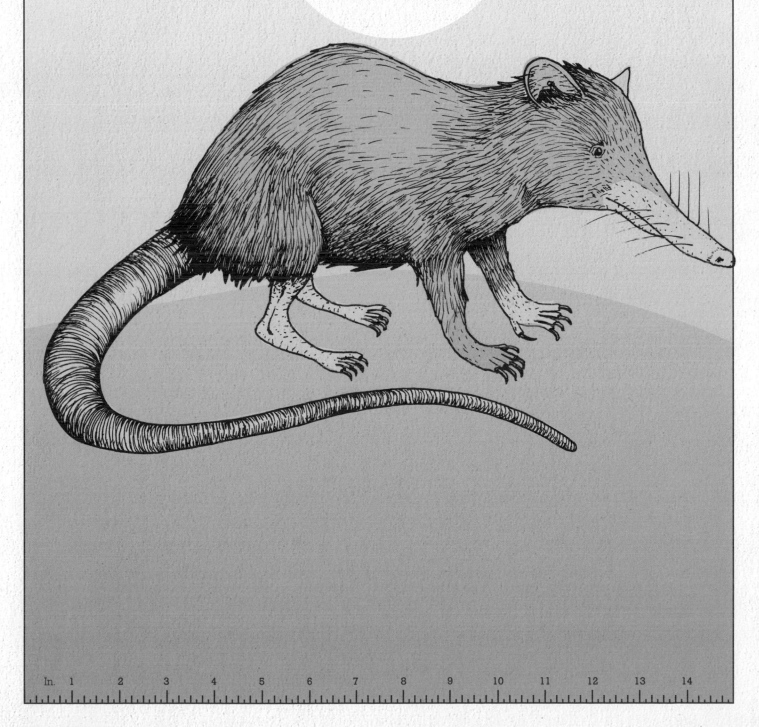

Fig. 71 Solenodon

The Hispaniolan
solenodon
has a very flexible snout.
The Hispaniolan solenodon's
snout even has a ball-and-socket
joint at its base, similar to the
human shoulder joint, to
increase its mobility.

In. 1   2   3   4   5   6   7   8   9   10   11   12   13   14

STAR-NOSED MOLE

SCIENTIFIC NAME: **CONDYLURA CRISTATA**

There's really no mistaking this unusual creature. But just in case you weren't sure, the star-nosed mole can be easily identified by the 22 fleshy tentacles protruding from its snout. It uses these appendages to feel its way around, and to identify food such as worms, insects, and crustaceans. This comes in extra handy considering the star-nosed mole is essentially blind. This little animal also happens to be an excellent swimmer and can propel itself along the bottoms of streams and ponds in search of food. It has recently been discovered that the star-nosed mole blows bubbles underwater, pushing the bubbles just far enough to touch the surface of whatever it is trying to identify, and then sucks the bubbles back into its nose. That way, it can sniff underwater!

SPEED EATER

It has been reported that the star-nosed mole is the fastest-eating mammal on the planet, taking less than $1/5$ of a second to identify and devour each item. Perhaps it should consider entering the Coney Island hot dog eating competition?

KINGDOM	**Animalia**
PHYLUM	**Chordata**
CLASS	**Mammalia**
ORDER	**Soricomorpha**
FAMILY	**Talpidae**
GENUS	**Condylura**
SPECIES	**C. cristata**

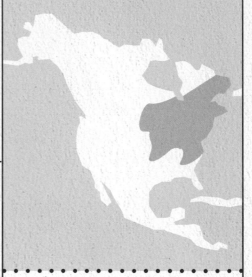

Distribution:
Eastern Canada and the northeastern United States.

Did you know?

The star-nosed mole has more than 25,000 sensory receptors distributed among its 11 sets of nose appendages.

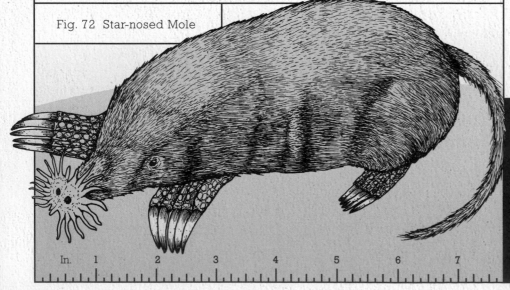

Fig. 72 Star-nosed Mole

In. 1 2 3 4 5 6 7

TAPIR

KINGDOM	**Animalia**
PHYLUM	**Chordata**
CLASS	**Mammalia**
ORDER	**Perissodactyla**
FAMILY	**Tapiridae**
GENUS	**Tapirus**
SPECIES	**Various**

SCIENTIFIC NAME: **TAPIRUS TERRESTRIS (AND OTHERS)**

It's easy to assume that the tapir might be some sort of pig with a trunk, or even a cousin of the anteater, but the fact is that this odd-toed ungulate is more closely related to horses and rhinoceroses. FYI, the term *odd-toed ungulate* is given to grazing animals whose hooves feature an odd number of toes (e.g., 1 or 3). But yes, the tapir does have a trunk, which helps it grab branches and delicious fruit. Tapirs are fast and agile, and like to create paths through the brush, which they share with other tapirs to help keep track of feeding grounds and water holes. They are excellent swimmers and can even dive to feed on underwater plants. Tapirs have been around for millions of years, and scientists believe they have changed very little over this time. At least 9 species of tapir have existed on the planet, but due to hunting and habitat destruction, only 4 remain, all of which are endangered.

Distribution:
South America,
Central America,
and Southeast Asia.

Did you know?

The **tapir** can use its nose like a snorkel while swimming.

Fig. 73 Tapir

Feet 1 2 3 4 5 6

TARDIGRADE

SCIENTIFIC NAME: **ECHINISCUS TESTUDO (AND OTHERS)**

The tardigrade is a water-dwelling, microscopic animal that can be found just about everywhere on the planet: from the very top of Mount Everest and 10,000 feet below the surface of the ocean to the ice fields of Antarctica and water droplets in your backyard! This eight-legged (and clawed) creature is one of the world's toughest animals. It can survive 1,000 times more radiation than any other animal, as well as temperatures of over 300°F and under -400°F.

KINGDOM	**Animalia**
PHYLUM	**Tardigrada**
CLASS	**Various**
ORDER	**Various**
FAMILY	**Various**
GENUS	**Various**
SPECIES	**Various**

Distribution: Water worldwide.

Did you know?

In 2007, tardigrades were taken into orbit on the *Foton-M3* space mission and exposed to the airless, gravityless vacuum of outer space. After they returned to Earth 10 days later, it was discovered that not only had they survived, but they had also laid eggs.

When things get too hot or too cold, or just too nasty, the tardigrade has the amazing ability to retract its legs and shed 96 to 98 percent of the water from its body, allowing it to shrivel up into a "cryptobiotic state," where it is more or less temporarily dead. Then, when conditions get better (perhaps 9 to 10 years later), it can regenerate and come back to life.

TRUE OR FALSE?

1 Tardigrades can grow up to 23 feet in length.

2 The tardigrade was first discovered in 1773.

3 If a tardigrade enters your ear, it is likely to whisper gibberish, which over time can lessen your intelligence.

4 Tardigrades come in a variety of colors, including white, red, orange, yellow, green, purple, black, and transparent.

5 A German candy company, Haribo, plans to release a line of eight-limbed, gummy tardigrades in the near future. It is speculated that the chewables will also be able to survive extreme levels of heat, cold, and radiation.

Answers: 1. F, 2. T, 3. F, 4. T, 5. F (But they should!)

Fig. 74 Tardigrade, water shedded.

Did you know?

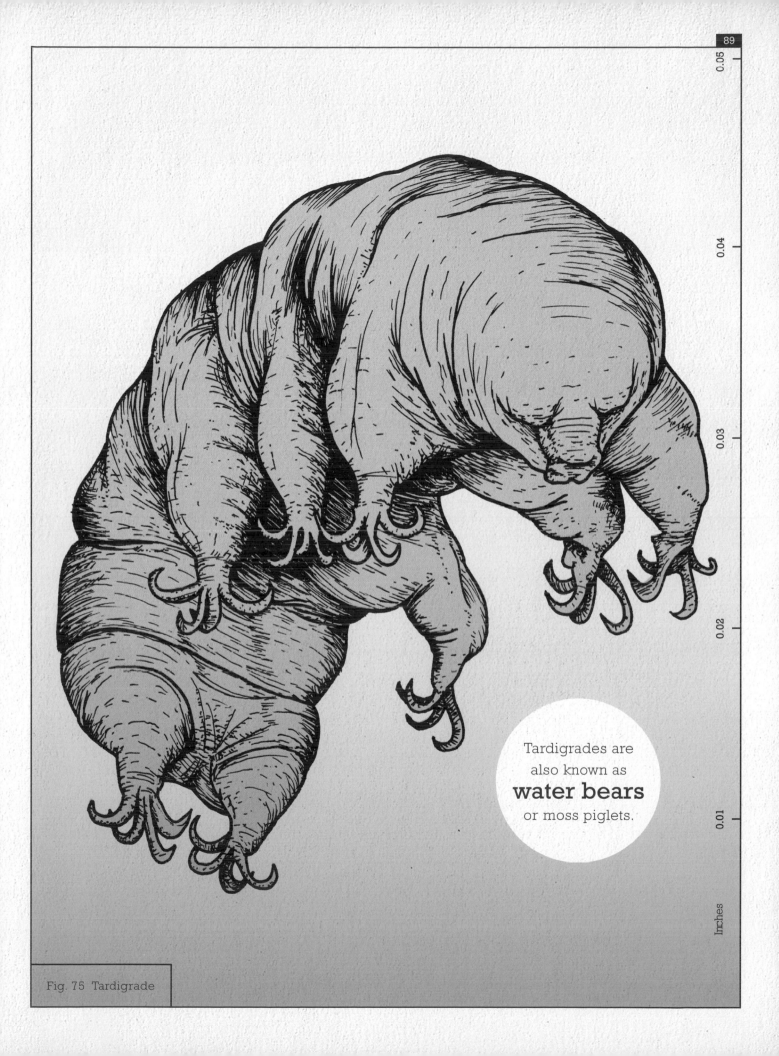

0.05

0.04

0.03

0.02

Tardigrades are
also known as
water bears
or moss piglets.

0.01

Inches

Fig. 75 Tardigrade

TEXAS HORNED LIZARD

SCIENTIFIC NAME: **PHRYNOSOMA CORNUTUM**

Don't mess with Texas! Okay, you can mess with Texas. But maybe don't mess with the Texas horned lizard. True to its name, this creature has a crown of horns adorning its head, as well as numerous spines across its back, which provide it with one serious coat of armor. But what makes this particular reptile so incredibly unusual is its ability to squirt a stream of blood from the corners of its eyes! Not only does this defense mechanism confuse its potential predators, but the blood also contains a chemical that tastes bad to dogs, wolves, and coyotes. Back off, pooch!

KINGDOM	**Animalia**
PHYLUM	**Chordata**
CLASS	**Sauropsida**
ORDER	**Squamata**
FAMILY	**Phrynosomatidae**
GENUS	**Phrynosoma**
SPECIES	**P. cornutum**

Did you know?

Fig. 76 The Texas horned lizard can squirt blood from its eye to a distance of up to 5 feet.

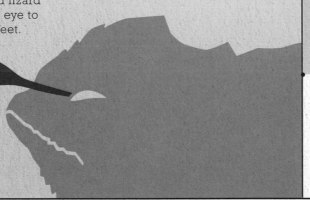

Distribution:
Colorado and Kansas to northern Mexico, and from southeastern Arizona to Texas.

SECOND LINE OF DEFENSE

In case squirting blood doesn't stop the enemy, when under attack the Texas horned lizard will puff itself up, causing its spiny scales to stick out even farther, making it a rather undesirable meal to swallow.

Fig. 77 Texas Horned Lizard

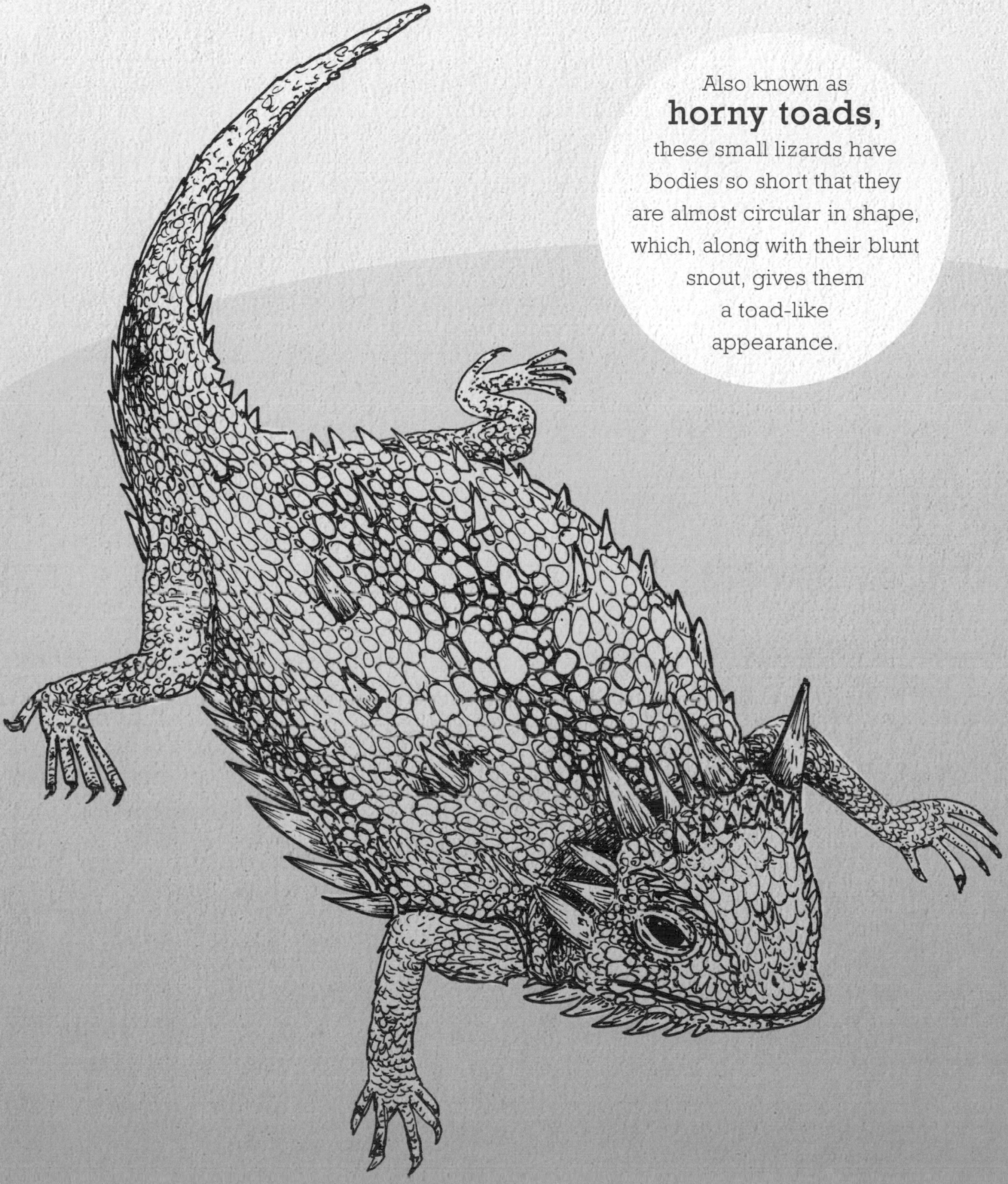

Also known as
horny toads,
these small lizards have bodies so short that they are almost circular in shape, which, along with their blunt snout, gives them a toad-like appearance.

1
2
3
4
5
Inches

THREE-TOED SLOTH

SCIENTIFIC NAME: **BRADYPUS VARIEGATUS (AND OTHERS)**

Congratulations, three-toed sloth, you are the world's slowest mammal! This creature is so slow that algae actually grows on its fur during the rainy season. Of course, this only helps it stay hidden while hanging upside down from trees in the rain forest. Three-toed sloths are about the size of a large house cat (with the exception of the pygmy three-toed sloth, which is more like, um, the size of a small house cat). They are arboreal, which means that they live in trees, typically in the lower branches. Sloths even sleep in trees, too, and they sleep a *lot*, like 15 to 20 hours a day. Even when they are awake they often remain motionless . . . which is why algae grows on their fur.

KINGDOM	**Animalia**
PHYLUM	**Chordata**
CLASS	**Mammalia**
ORDER	**Pilosa**
FAMILY	**Bradypodidae**
GENUS	**Bradypus**
SPECIES	**Various**

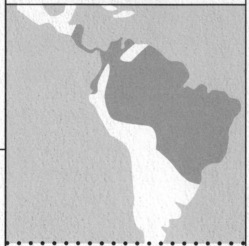

Distribution:
South and Central America.

Fig. 78 Three-toed sloth eating.

THREE-TOED SLOTH FACTS

1 There are four species of three-toed sloth: the pale-throated three-toed sloth, the brown-throated three-toed sloth, the maned three-toed sloth, and the pygmy three-toed sloth, all of which live in the trees of Central and South America.

2 Sloths travel at a top speed of about 0.15 miles per hour. In other words, it would take a sloth almost a half hour to run the bases of a major league baseball diamond.

3 The hair on a sloth curves in the opposite direction of most other mammals: from the stomach to the back. Clearly, this is a mohawk waiting to happen.

Did you know?

Sloths are identified by the number of long curved claws that they have on each front foot. (There are also two-toed sloths.)

Fig. 79 Three-Toed Sloth

2

1

Feet

TIBURONIA GRANROJO
(BIG RED JELLYFISH)

SCIENTIFIC NAME: **TIBURONIA GRANROJO**

There's something fantastic about the fact that humans have inhabited Earth for 200 thousand years, and we're still discovering new creatures, including species of jellyfish, which were around for 500 million years before we got here. The massive *Tiburonia granrojo* jellyfish was identified in 2003 in the deep waters off the coast of California. Spanning between 2 and 10 feet (yes, a 10-foot-wide jellyfish), and living up to a mile below the surface, the Tiburonia is especially unusual because of its lack of tentacles. Instead, between 4 and 7 short, stocky arms protrude from its massive red body. This discovery forced scientists to come up with an entirely new subfamily of jellyfish—Tiburoniinae, named after the Tiburon ROV (an underwater vehicle), which they were using when they discovered this jellyfish. Unfortunately, at the moment, not a lot else is known about Big Red. Please check back soon . . .

KINGDOM	**Animalia**
PHYLUM	**Cnidaria**
CLASS	**Scyphozoa**
ORDER	**Semaeostomeae**
FAMILY	**Ulmaridae**
GENUS	**Tiburonia**
SPECIES	**T. granrojo**

FACTS ABOUT THE TIBURONIA GRANROJO AND OTHER JELLYFISH

1 Jellyfish do not have a heart, bones, or a brain. They do, however, have lots and lots of nerves.

2 Jellyfish are typically made up of about 95 percent water.

3 *Granrojo* means "big red" in Spanish, but maybe you already figured that out.

4 Jellyfish diets typically consist of smaller fish and zooplankton. This is thought to be the case for the *Tiburonia granrojo* as well.

5 All jellyfish sting, injecting venom into their prey, but only some species have a sting that will cause an adverse reaction in humans.

6 In the last 20 years, scientists have discovered more than 50 new species of jellies.

Distribution: Across the Pacific Ocean in the Sea of Cortez, Monterey Bay, and waters around Hawaii and Japan.

The largest jellyfish on the planet is the lion's mane jellyfish. It can grow up to 120 feet in length . . . arguably the longest animal on the planet.

Did you know?

Fig. 80 Tiburonia Granrojo

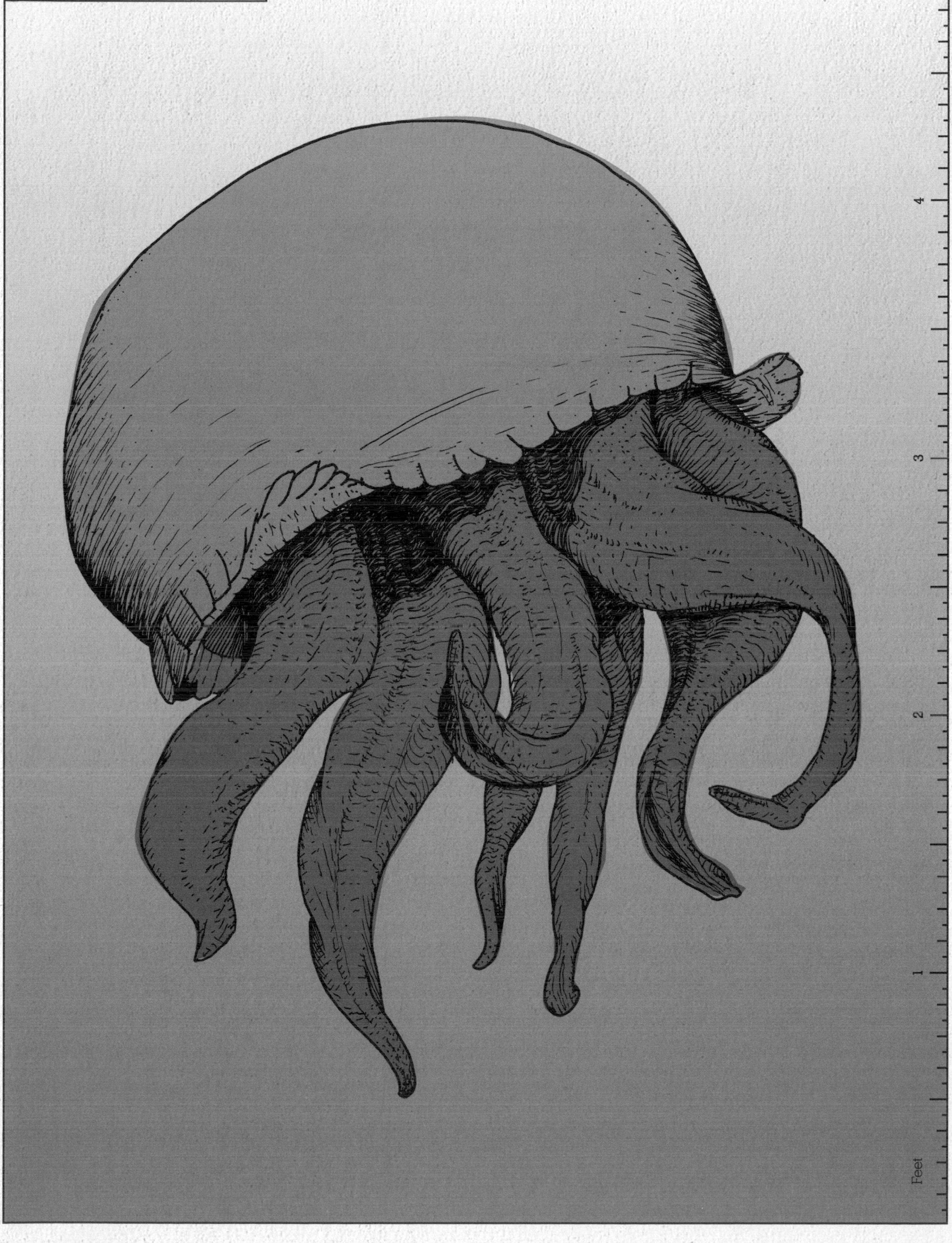

WEDDELL SEAL

SCIENTIFIC NAME: **LEPTONYCHOTES WEDDELLII**

The Weddell seal lives farther south than any other mammal, inhabiting parts of Antarctica that are within 800 miles of the South Pole. This pinniped (which is a fancy way of saying "fin-footed creature") can grow over 9 feet in length and can weigh more than 1,200 pounds. It can also dive over 2,000 feet deep and stay submerged for over an hour. But what really makes the Weddell seal so incredibly unusual are the sounds it makes both above and below the ice. The easiest way to know what they sound like is to imagine the sounds of laser beams being fired, or light sabers being swung in the *Star Wars* movies. The next easiest way (or perhaps it's easier) is to go to the website Antarctica2000.net and listen to samples recorded by Douglas Quin, PhD, who traveled to Antarctica on several occasions and recorded the sounds of this amazing animal using a pair of hydrophones (underwater microphones).

KINGDOM	**Animalia**
PHYLUM	**Chordata**
CLASS	**Mammalia**
ORDER	**Carnivora**
FAMILY	**Phocidae**
GENUS	**Leptonychotes**
SPECIES	**L. weddellii**

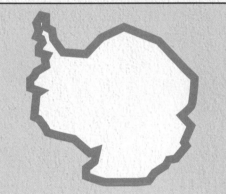

Distribution:
The coast of Antarctica.

Did you know?

Humans can easily approach Weddell seals. The hard part is getting to Antarctica.

FEEDING FACTOID

Weddell seals mainly feed upon fish, squid, and krill. They have been known to blow air into cracks in the ice to flush out small fish.

Fig. 81

Fig. 82 Weddell Seal

The
Weddell seal
was "discovered" in
the 1820s by a British
explorer named James Weddell.
Unfortunately for the seals,
James Weddell also
happened to be a seal
hunter.

Feet   1   2   3   4   5

WOMBAT

KINGDOM	**Animalia**
PHYLUM	**Chordata**
CLASS	**Mammalia**
ORDER	**Diprotodontia**
FAMILY	**Vombatidae**
GENUS	**Various**
SPECIES	**Various**

SCIENTIFIC NAME: **LASIORHINUS KREFFTII (AND OTHERS)**

Native only to Australia, wombats are short-legged, muscular, nocturnal marsupials that look somewhat like a combination of a pig and a bear. Wombats are herbivores, feeding on grasses, herbs, bark, and roots. They have a very slow metabolism—it takes around 8 to 14 days to complete digestion—which helps them survive multiple days in a hot and arid environment. When they are ready, their feces comes out in a cuboid shape. In other words, the wombat poops cubes!

THE SCOOP ON WOMBAT POOP

Distribution: Tasmania and the southern coast of mainland Australia.

How do they manage to create cubed poop? Wombats have special bones in their backsides that allow them to squeeze and form their feces into a special six-sided shape.

Why do they do this? So that the poop doesn't roll away! Wombats often defecate on the tops of rocks and logs to help mark the path home. They don't want their trail markers to roll off into the leaves.

What else is wombat poop good for? Somehow a company in Tasmania called the Creative Paper Company has found a way to make paper out of wombat scat. It's been a hit with tourists looking for Australian souvenirs. Apparently the paper has "a nice organic smell."

Fig. 83 Square wombat poop.

Did you know?

An unofficial Wombat Day is observed on October 22, at the beginning of the traditional spring planting season.

Fig. 84 Wombat

Even though **wombats** are native only to Australia, most Australians have never seen a wild wombat.

Feet   1   2

YETI CRAB

SCIENTIFIC NAME: KIWA HIRSUTA

Just discovered in 2005, in the South Pacific Ocean, the yeti crab is a blind deep-sea crustacean whose legs are covered with long, thin yellow hairs. It is approximately 6 inches in length and lives at a depth of 7,200 feet. (That's almost 6 times deeper than the height of the Empire State Building.) Because this crab is so different from anything biologists have seen before, a whole new family of animal had to be created to classify it—Kiwaidae, which comes from the Latin word for "hairy." Although there is much to be learned about this crab, scientists believe that the purpose of the hair on the crab's legs is for trapping bacteria, which the crab may use as food. But this is merely one theory. Perhaps you can come up with your own?

KINGDOM	**Animalia**
PHYLUM	**Arthropoda**
CLASS	**Malacostraca**
ORDER	**Decapoda**
FAMILY	**Kiwaidae**
GENUS	**Kiwa**
SPECIES	**K. hirsuta**

Distribution:
South Pacific Ocean.

DISCOVERY OF THE YETI CRAB

In March of 2005, the yeti crab was discovered not far from Easter Island, in the South Pacific. The team that discovered the crab was conducting deep-ocean research to explore hydrothermal vents along the Pacific-Antarctic ridge. (Hydrothermal vents are basically hot water geysers along the seafloor.) During one particular submarine dive, a marine biologist noticed an unusually large crab with hairy arms crawling across the seafloor. The crab was captured and brought back to the surface. Over the course of several more dives, the researchers started to see more and more of these crabs, hiding behind rocks, with just the tips of their arms sticking out. After returning to the shore, researchers in Spain helped identify the newly discovered crab, giving it the family name Kiwaidae, and the species name *Kiwa hirsuta*. Of course, "yeti crab" is much more fun to say.

Yeti versus Yeti crab

Is it real?   It's real!

Fig. 85 Because of its furry legs, this animal was nicknamed the "yeti crab," after the yeti, or abominable snowman of the Himalayas. Of course, there is no proof that the abominable snowman actually exists, unlike the yeti crab.

Fig. 86 Yeti Crab

YOU KNOW WHAT MAKES ME SAD?

I'll tell you what makes me sad: an animal that's been around for millions of years suddenly going extinct . . . because of us! Go ahead, look up the Tasmanian tiger—check out a photo of this amazing creature. Thanks to humans, this animal is now extinct. Gone forever. Here are a few other animals that have disappeared from the face of our planet in just the past century: the Caribbean monk seal, the golden toad, the passenger pigeon, the Tecopa pupfish, the Baiji River dolphin, the Bubal Hartebeest antelope, and, most likely, the West African black rhino.

Why do animals go extinct? Well, sometimes it's totally out of our control (like the giant meteorite that crashed into Earth 65 million years ago and wiped out the dinosaurs), but the vast majority of extinctions, at least in the past 100 years, are because of humans. We have a problem. We can't stop throwing trash into the ocean, cutting down forests, spraying chemicals into the air, overfishing, and, in general, taking way more than we need. This behavior affects all of the animals on our planet, including us. We can, however, live more conscientiously by not taking as much from Earth. Here are some things you can do to help keep a few unusual (and usual) creatures alive:

A FEW CLOSING WORDS

USE LESS ENERGY

• Take public transportation if it's available. Walk or ride a bicycle when possible.

• Replace your regular light bulbs with new compact fluorescent bulbs. Yes, the color of the light is not so great. But the Sun's color won't be either when we no longer have an atmosphere.

• Turn off lights, computers, and the TV when you are not using them.

• Adjust your thermostat just a few degrees warmer in the summer, and a few degrees colder in the winter.

• Hang your clothes out to dry.

• Buy local food. Think about how much energy it takes to get food imported from far away. (On that note, maybe eat just a little less meat. Try eating vegetarian just one day a week!)

• Wash your clothes in warm water instead of hot water. I promise, they'll still get clean.

TASMANIAN TIGER

WE'RE SORRY THIS ANIMAL NO LONGER EXISTS

USE LESS WATER

- Got a dishwasher? Don't rinse your dishes before putting them in.

- Turn off the water while you brush your teeth.

- Take slightly shorter showers. Take baths less often.

- Use water-saving devices on your toilet, taps, and showerhead.

USE LESS STUFF

- Chill out with the plastic bags and bottled water! Seriously. Get yourself a couple reusable nylon/fabric bags and take them with you every time you shop. Instead of buying bottles of water, get a filter for your faucet. If you absolutely need spring water, buy it in large containers, and be sure to recycle the jugs.

- Use less paper. It comes from trees, and animals live in trees. Get a printer that prints on both sides of the paper, and don't print unless you have to.

- Use fewer napkins and paper towels. You don't need a huge stack of napkins at the fast-food joint. (Actually, you don't need fast food, either.)

- Cut down on junk mail. There are specific groups you can call, such as 885-5-OPTOUT, for credit card solicitations.

- Buy products and food without packaging whenever possible. Learn to love the bulk bins.

- Parents: Use cloth diapers (or at least environmentally friendly diapers).

- Use rechargeable batteries.

- Before you throw something away, think about whether someone else might want it.

- Recycle! Don't be lazy. You can do it.

Share your knowledge with others. Tell them about the amazing animals in our world and explain why many are endangered. Encourage others to learn more.

TEN ORGANIZATIONS YOU SHOULD KNOW

World Wildlife Fund www.worldwildlife.org

The Nature Conservancy www.nature.org

Wildlife Conservation Society www.wcs.org

Natural Resources Defense Council www.nrdc.org

The Endangered Species Program www.fws.gov/endangered

RARE Conservation www.rareconservation.org

Oceana www.oceana.org

National Wildlife Federation www.nwf.org

Conservation International www.conservation.org

Audubon Society www.audubon.org

OH, ONE MORE THING!

I have a website. Actually, I have a bunch of websites:
www.michaelhearst.com, www.oneringzero.com, www.songsforicecreamtrucks.com,
but the one I really want to share with you is: www.unusualcreatures.com.
Here you can see more images and videos, learn more fun facts, and take more quizzes.

And while you're at it, you can buy a copy of *Songs for Unusual Creatures,*
an album of instrumental songs for kids *and* adults, featuring the Kronos Quartet,
the Microscopic Septet, Margaret Leng Tan, the League of Electronic Musical Urban Robots,
and some of the strangest musical instruments you've never heard of!

Tracks include:
Blue-Footed Booby, Chinese Giant Salamander, Dugong,
Aye-Aye, Elephant Shrew, Glass Frog, Blobfish, Honey Badger,
Magnapinna Squid, Tardigrade, Anglerfish, Jesus Christ Lizard,
Bilby, and Weddell Seal.

Might I also suggest you visit:
www.elasticbrand.net to see some of Arjen Noordeman
and Christie Wright's other amazing design work, and
www.jelmernoordeman.com to check out Jelmer
Noordeman's other excellent illustrations.

By the way, this book is dedicated to Easton, Felix, Greta, and Opal.

Huge thanks to Joe Beshenkovsky, Jason Bitner, Linsey Bostwick, Cecilia Brauer, Paul Cohen, Peter Comber, Duke Lemur Center, Kelly Eudailey, Claudia Gonson, Lari Hatley, David Harrington and the Kronos Quartet, Philip Johnston and the Microscopic Septet, Andrea Katz, Jud Laghi, Eloise Leigh, Fiona Maazel, Melissa Manlove, Ellen Mendlow, Steve Mockus, Sharon Price, Douglas Quin, Doug Quint, Eric Singer and the League of Electronic Musical Urban Robots, Alan Rapp, RARE Conservation, Wade Schuman, Glenn Shea, Margaret Leng Tan, Kevin Tkacz, Julia Vasker Zeltser, Kimberly Weatherell, Maia Weinstock, Peter Wright, and Anne Yoder.

And a big thank-you to all the Kickstarter backers who donated enough money to get their name in print right here! Susanne Ahmari, Max, Otto, and Rachel Allard, Alimentum-The Literature of Food, Anonymous, Charlie Atherton, Erik Banner, the Bears, Jenny Benevento, Ben jammin, Shuli Berger, Ina Bergmann, Michael Bernholtz, Joe Beshenkovsky, Dina Bisagna, Danielle and Jason Bitner, Blight Productions, Jenny Block, Tara Bloyd, Mathilde Bouhon, Andy Busch, David Cabianca, Bill Carey, Ilina Chaudhuri, Colette, Communist Prime, María Correas, Astrid Cravens, Marcin Cybula, Bret Dahlgren, Laura de Sae-Silva, Dennis DiClaudio, Laurie E., Betsy & Forrest Eudailey, Kelly Eudailey, Michael Fagan, Melissa Farran, Jimmy Frazier, Alina Fridberg, Karen Gerard, Will Gilfillan, Claudia Gonson, Alex Graf, Daniel Graf, Tatiana Graf, Sanae Guerin, Matthea Harvey, Earl Hearst, Jeanie Hearst, the Heggosaurs, Claire Heitlinger, John Hodgman, Phil and Ruth Holmes, Carol Hooker, the Hotts, Lisa Irene, Stacy Irwin, Jonathan Israel, Leslie Kaplan, Rachel Keene Esser, Mai Kiigemagi, Sarah Klein, Jonathan Kohrs, Jean Kottemann, Jessica Lamb-Shapiro, Christine Lambert, Melanie Landau, Frank Language, Paulette Licitra, Fiona Maazel, Mr. Colin MacKenzie, Tara MacNamara, Jennifer McClory, Tina McMullen, Amy McNamara, Robert Meganck, The Ministry of Information, Rick Moody, M.J. Moriarty, Cynthia Mumford, Patrick, Clare Neylan Parfitt, Paul Pazniokas, Lauren Petty, Nicki Pombier Berger, Heidi Reinberg, Martin Rathgeber, Sam, Schmooley, John Sell, Julie Shapiro, Alex Sherwin, Julie, Eliott, and Ethan Shrack, Jason Akira Somma, Patrick Stallbaumer, Kate Steciw, Sara Steenrod, Rebecca Stern, Michael Stockelman, Shanta Thake, Stephanie Thompson, Hayden's TiaMija, Theron Trowbridge, Elisabeth van Aerde, Erik Van Wyck, Victoria Welch, Lily Yang, Irene Ziegler Aston, and Jeramy L. Zimmerman.

Let's not forget Ron Caswell, Brian Drye, Ben Holmes, Allyssa Lamb, and Kristin Mueller, who play music with me and wear unusual creature costumes in front of an audience.

Another round of applause for Arjen Noordeman and Christie Wright (aka Elasticbrand) who have stuck with me and gone way above and beyond. Thank you!

ABOUT THE AUTHOR:

Michael Hearst is a composer, multi-instrumentalist, and writer. He is a founding member of the band One Ring Zero, which has released nine albums, including *Planets*, *Wake Them Up*, the book/CDs *As Smart As We Are (The Author Project)*, and *The Recipe Project*. Hearst's solo works include *Songs for Ice Cream Trucks* and *Songs for Unusual Creatures*, as well as the soundtracks for the movies *The Good Mother*, *The House of Suh*, and *Magic Camp*. He lives in Brooklyn, where just about everything he needs is within a four-block radius.

ABOUT THE DESIGNERS:

Arjen Noordeman and Christie Wright work together as the multi-disciplinary studio Elasticbrand, designing media and products for clients in the arts and entertainment sectors. Arjen has worked as an art director for several broadcast organizations including Nickelodeon (NYC) and held the position of director of design at the Massachusetts Museum of Contemporary Art. Christie has created work for publications including *Martha Stewart Living* and *Bloom*, for trend forecasting company Studio Edelkoort (France), and for West Elm (NYC). She is currently head of brand design for Marcel Wanders, studio (Netherlands). Elasticbrand's "Audiowear" porcelain musical jewelry was recently acquired by the Museum of Arts and Design (NYC).

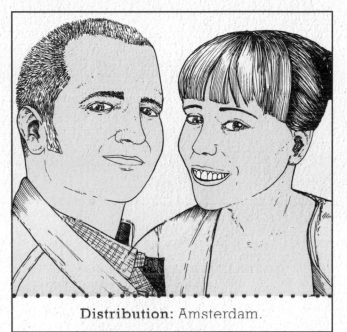

Distribution: Amsterdam.

Distribution: Brooklyn.

ABOUT THE ILLUSTRATOR:

Jelmer Noordeman is an independent illustrator based in Rotterdam. He has created projects for Diesel and KRO television, among others. His autonomous work has been exhibited in numerous Dutch and international galleries. As co-founder of ZWARD (his design studio with Kirsten Spuijbroek), he most recently presented a jewelry collection inspired by toys at Dutch Design Week. He is a member of the artist collective Bier en Brood, and is a 2010 Willem DeKooning Maaskant Award and Drempelprijs (Threshold) Award nominee. Jelmer also happens to be Arjen's brother.

Distribution: Rotterdam.

INDEX